SUTHERLAND QUARTERLY

SQ

Sutherland Quarterly is an exciting new series
of captivating essays on current affairs
by some of Canada's finest writers,
published individually as books
and also available by annual subscription.

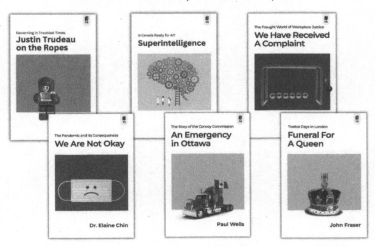

Governing in Troubled Times
Justin Trudeau on the Ropes

Is Canada Ready for AI?
Superintelligence

The Fraught World of Workplace Justice
We Have Received A Complaint

The Pandemic and its Consequences
We Are Not Okay
Dr. Elaine Chin

The Story of the Convoy Commission
An Emergency in Ottawa
Paul Wells

Twelve Days in London
Funeral For A Queen
John Fraser

SUBSCRIBE ONLINE AT
SUTHERLANDQUARTERLY.COM

SUPERINTELLIGENCE

SUPERINTELLIGENCE

Is Canada Ready for AI?

REPORTED BY THE LOGIC

SQ

Sutherland House
416 Moore Ave., Suite 205
Toronto, ON M4G 1C9

First edition, February 2024

If you are interested in inviting one of our authors to a live event or
media appearance, please contact sranasinghe@sutherlandhousebooks.com
and visit our website at sutherlandhousebooks.com for more
information about our authors and their schedules.

We acknowledge the support of the Government of Canada.

Manufactured in Canada
Cover designed by Jordan Lunn
Cover elements from Freepik, iStock, and Alamy
Book composed by Karl Hunt

Library and Archives Canada Cataloguing in Publication
Title: Superintelligence : is Canada ready for AI? / reported by The Logic.
Names: Logic (Newsroom), author.
Description: Series statement: Sutherland quarterly ; 5 | Includes bibliographical references.
Identifiers: Canadiana (print) 20230593402 | Canadiana (ebook) 20230593496 |
ISBN 9781990823633 (softcover) | ISBN 9781990823640 (EPUB)
Subjects: LCSH: Artificial intelligence—Technological innovations—Canada. |
LCSH: Artificial intelligence—Social aspects—Canada. | LCSH: Artificial intelligence—
Economic aspects—Canada.
Classification: LCC Q335 .L64 2024 | DDC 006.30971—dc23

ISBN 978-1-990823-63-3
eBook 978-1-990823-64-0

CONTENTS

CONTENTS

ABOUT THE AUTHOR

The Logic is Canada's business and technology newsroom, globally recognized for its award-winning, original reporting. Founded in 2018, the publication provides in-depth reporting on the organizations, policies, and people driving Canada's economy.

This compilation of stories written by the reporters of The Logic was edited by Charlie Gillis, April Fong, Jordan Timm, and Mark Stevenson.

Fact-checking, copyediting, and production by Hanna Lee, Sebastian Leck, Sumaiya Kamani, and Aaliyah Dasoo.

INTRODUCTION

When the Lumière brothers debuted the first motion picture film in 1895, it was an engineering marvel. Legend has it that the fifty-second film showing a train steamrolling towards the camera felt so realistic for members of the audience that they jumped out of their seats.

Despite that initial success, it would take another twenty-six years for Charlie Chaplin to direct *The Kid*, which popularized feature-length motion pictures. Sound in cinema would take another five years, virtual reality headsets another 116.

While neural networks were proposed as far back as 1944, it wasn't until a 1986 paper co-authored by the British-Canadian computer scientist Geoffrey Hinton, then a professor at Carnegie Mellon University, that the practical idea of a neural network was first born. It would take another twenty-six years for Hinton, by then at the University of Toronto, and two graduate students to turn that idea into a deep learning artificial intelligence model able to scan thousands of photos and learn to identify common objects such as flowers, dogs, and cars.

While Moore's law suggests that innovative tech hardware accelerates exponentially, it is a striking coincidence that it took the same length of time for Chaplin to adopt moving picture technology for the masses as it did for Hinton to turn his research paper into an application that leapt off the page.

What's happened since has been nothing short of remarkable.

In effect, there is a time before November 30, 2022, and a time after. On that date, OpenAI released ChatGPT to the world, reaching 100 million monthly active users just two months after launch to make it the fastest-growing consumer application in history. The tool put the power of deep learning at anyone's fingertips, serving as teacher, coder, designer, author, and even romantic partner.

ChatGPT's launch set off a hype cycle that would've made purported Bitcoin creator Satoshi Nakamoto squirm, resulting in a funding frenzy

11

for AI startups, a race for "compute" power among tech giants, and promises of riches from LinkedIn self-promoters. Meanwhile, lawmakers around the world have raced to catch up to a technology that could either save or eradicate humankind, depending on whom you ask. The turmoil that engulfed OpenAI's leadership, which according to reports pitted CEO Sam Altman against Ilya Sutskever, the company's Canadian chief scientist, will only amplify the sense of urgency.

The Logic is Canada's business and technology newsroom. Founded in 2018, we publish agenda-setting reporting on the people and companies driving Canada's innovation economy. We're widely recognized for our coverage of the rise of Big Tech, the economic impact of sustainable investing, the Wild West of digital currencies, and the transformation of the auto industry, among other subjects.

Our team of journalists in bureaus across the country is focused on the question of what kind of country Canada wants to be. Through our in-depth investigative reporting and analysis, we start the hard conversations Canadians need to have if we want to compete on the global stage.

When Sutherland House approached us about a collaboration, we were excited to bring some of our work on AI to the printed page. This volume is built around the most deeply reported and ambitious editorial series in The Logic's more than five-year history.

In these pages, we tell the colourful story of how Canada found itself on the leading edge of AI research in the first place. We meet the country's current AI champions—and some fallen ones. We look at one industry where applying the technology has given Canadian companies a vital competitive edge, and at what's keeping other businesses from replicating that success. We examine how the technology is affecting workers in Canada, and how the country is navigating the fraught geopolitics of AI. We explore what a future infused with AI could feel like. We delve into how the brightest lights of Canadian AI research became fearful of its destructive potential, and how their fears have guided the world's policymakers. And we take you to Bletchley Park, site of last November's UK AI Safety Summit, to see how Canada and its AI champions measure up on the global stage.

Canada has played a key role in the AI revolution. We have funded the research, developed the neural networks, and although we are a relatively small country, we have created a first-mover advantage that other, larger nations should envy.

Will Canada succeed? Or will we follow a path that's all too familiar in this country, squandering our advantages in the face of global competition?

The deafening hype of the last year may make it seem that we've reached peak AI. The Lumière brothers and Charlie Chaplin show us this story has only just begun.

David Skok
Founder & Editor-in-Chief
The Logic
December 2023

CHAPTER ONE

FOUNDATIONS

By Murad Hemmadi

On a trip to California a few years ago, Ruslan Salakhutdinov made time to hang out with some old school chums. A decade earlier, the group had shared a lab at the University of Toronto—and a massive achievement.

Salakhutdinov and his lab mates had studied under Geoffrey Hinton, the celebrated exponent of deep learning. With colleagues around the country and the world, the professor and his pupils ushered in a series of innovations that enabled the modern field of artificial intelligence. Together, they thawed the neural-net winter, ending a period when their preferred AI approach—based on trying to mimic the way humans think—was out of favour and funding.

In doing so, they made possible the generative AI summer that the world is basking in today, as well as applications with society-changing potential, from faster drug discovery to climate solutions. AI now is red hot, everywhere from the meetings of world leaders to those of high school teachers.

By the time of the gathering in Silicon Valley, at least have the classmates were living in California, most working at companies such as Apple, Google, and OpenAI. Hinton was spending a portion of his time at Google. Salakhutdinov was in Pittsburgh, a professor at Carnegie Mellon University working on novel ways to structure the massive volumes of data many AI models need. Their story of shared vision, success, and exit is an all too familiar tale for Canada.

Although few people noticed as it was happening, Hinton's group, along with peers in Montreal and Edmonton, had made Canada, for a time, the place to build AI.

Take the internet's favourite new toy: ChatGPT, launched in November, 2022. The viral query-response system from San Francisco-based OpenAI gave many ordinary people their first encounter with a machine that felt intelligent. Its arrival signalled that everyday AI could be a fact of the present rather than a science-fiction future. "There's almost like a pre-ChatGPT world and post-ChatGPT world," Innovation Minister François-Philippe Champagne observed at a robot-habited AI conference in September 2023.

ChatGPT was born in California, but crucial parts of its lineage trace back to Canada. Chief scientist Ilya Sutskever—a lynchpin member of the OpenAI board that recently ousted, then reinstated, CEO Sam Altman—once shared a U of T lab with Salakhutdinov. Dozens of other staff at OpenAI are drawn from top Canadian schools. The transformer approach that puts the "T" on ChatGPT came from a June 2017 paper co-authored by a group of Google researchers, including Canadian Aidan Gomez. And the whole superstructure of text- and image-generating tools rests on the deep learning foundations laid in Canadian labs over the last two decades.

That goes for much of modern AI. Canadian researchers demonstrated how the technology could work; many went on to the tech titans and challengers now putting it to work. Startups and scale-ups across the US and elsewhere are now looking to develop AI's next world-changing, money-spinning application. That the initial work has deep roots in Canada and so much of the economic opportunity is being realized elsewhere strikes many observers as a missed opportunity.

Canada has held, and lost, the global lead on technologies before, watching corporate champions such as Nortel and BlackBerry rise and fall. To benefit from the AI boom, the country will need to better capitalize on its inventions and keep its commercial contenders on track. Firms will need to compete with better resourced rivals for the talented people who will drive AI forward—like the ones who once clustered around Hinton at U of T.

While Canada's place in the grand AI show is far from assured, the country is hardly a poor player today. Some of our current champions of the technology rank among the world's best.

Gomez's startup, Toronto-headquartered Cohere, is racing against OpenAI to get tech giants, corporate behemoths and new ventures to use its large language models (LLMs) to produce content and summarize text. The firm has raised US$440 million, per PitchBook data, and in August

2023 was valued at US$3 billion in a deal involving its stock. (OpenAI has raised more than US$11 billion and has a valuation at least eight times that.)

Cohere is not alone. Toronto-based Ada is using LLMs for customer-service automation tools. Quebec City's Coveo is using them for search. Another Toronto firm, Ideogram, is building models that make images.

There is more to AI than large language models. Canadian startups are applying machine learning to all sorts of applications: AbCellera, BenchSci, and Congruence to drug discovery; Certn to background checks; Dcbel to home-energy management; Mindbridge to auditing; and Sanctuary AI to robots.

"The ecosystem that I'm in [is] still super nascent," says Gomez, whose firm is arguably Canada's current AI champion. "I want to see tens, hundreds of Toronto- or Canada-based AI companies."

Canada may not produce a Nortel or a BlackBerry—a single, world-beating AI company. But given how those stories ended, the economy may be better served by a portfolio of firms competing at the forefront of different fields.

Plenty are working to join that pack. Firms large and small are filling their offices with machine-learning engineers and data scientists from the same schools where the field's modern methods were invented.

AI enthusiasts elsewhere are keen to join them, says Foteini Agrafioti, head of RBC's Borealis AI lab. She notes that a class at the IITs, India's network of prestige engineering schools, might spend an entire semester implementing a paper out of the Vector Institute for Artificial Intelligence, a Toronto-based not-for-profit corporation dedicated to AI research. "So they're thinking, 'That's the destination.'" Salakhutdinov, for one, figures he might have stayed in Toronto had the Vector Institute, launched with federal, provincial, and corporate funding in 2017, existed when he exited in February 2016.

Dozens of executives, founders, and researchers interviewed by The Logic cited the quality of Canada's AI workforce as a strength. "There are very few places in the world that produce more of this talent than Montreal and Toronto," says Steven Woods, a partner at VC firm Inovia Capital and former longtime Google executive.

But the country's economic history provides plenty of cautionary tales of resources—human or material—ceded to other places, or simply squandered.

BlackBerry, for instance, blew its own chance with AI. In the summer of 2009, the Waterloo firm was still a technology titan, its clickety keyboards thumbed everywhere from Wall Street trading floors to the Oval Office. In Toronto that same season, Hinton's students built a model to predict phonemes—the base unit of meaning in speech—from sound waves.

The result was speech recognition better than anything the corporate world had been able to produce in three decades of research and development.

Tech giants Microsoft and IBM scooped up two of Hinton's ingenious students as interns. A third, Navdeep Jaitly, sought a Canadian post. Hinton and his pupil approached the company then known as Research in Motion, later as BlackBerry. "We said, 'We've got this new way of doing speech recognition, and it works better than the existing technology,'" recounted Hinton at an October event hosted by the investment firm Radical Ventures. "We'd like a student to come to you over the summer to show you how to use it, and then you can have the best speech recognition in your cellphone."

RIM passed. "Our attempt to give it to Canadian industry failed," said Hinton. Jaitly went to Google, which built the speech-recognition technology into its Android operating system to take on Apple's smooth-toned Siri. The iPhone killed the BlackBerry. "It was a shame that Canadian industry didn't [adopt it]," Hinton says now. "I think we might have still had BlackBerrys if that had happened."

Canada and its AI companies hope to script a happier ending for the next tale about the country's technology sector. Woods, the venture capitalist, is optimistic. "We have a very great story here."

CHAPTER TWO

ROGUE TO VOGUE

By Murad Hemmadi

As the last millennium was giving way to this one, Philippe Beaudoin found himself among about a dozen people watching as a man at the front of a room unfurled a vision of a technology's future. "It was such a beautiful concept," recalls Beaudoin, whose voice seems designed to express wonder. "More like alchemy than mathematics and science."

Yoshua Bengio was the man, his Université de Montréal lecture hall the room, and artificial intelligence the technology. The concept was neural networks, a methodology modelled on the human brain. It was not in vogue at the time. "It was kind of rogue AI, almost," says Beaudoin, then a master's student.

Two short decades on, it is mainstream. Bengio and Geoffrey Hinton are now the most-cited AI researchers in the world, according to Google Scholar. Startups are raising billions to build AI systems based on neural networks. Giant corporations are pivoting and partnering to use and sell the technology. Policymakers the world over are scrambling to regulate it.

But moving from alchemy to ubiquitous technology takes time, talent, and not a little serendipity. In AI, Canada found itself with all three. A community of researchers led by Bengio and others dedicated to neural networks persevered through the skepticism of their computer science peers and proved them wrong. They trained a new generation of AI modelled on the mind, and a generation of bright minds that would keep advancing those models. A public research program backed the work, and an unpopular bet paid out spectacularly.

Researchers in Montreal, Toronto and beyond demonstrated how the technology could work. While many went on to the tech titans and challengers now putting AI to work. Beaudoin's Montreal-based Waverly is among the startups and scale-ups looking to develop AI's next world-changing, money-spinning application at home in Canada.

"Why are we Canadian?" says Nicholas Frosst, who co-founded Cohere with Aidan Gomez and Ivan Zhang. "'Cuz we are." To his mind, staying in Canada, avoiding the inexorable pull to the south, is no longer a radical choice. Cohere, which makes generative AI tools for business, has felt little pressure to make the leap to Silicon Valley. "It turns out a lot of people want to be in Toronto," says Frosst.

The same is true for emerging AI companies in Montreal, Edmonton, and Vancouver, and plenty of points in between. There is no shortage of founders, researchers, and policymakers who insist Canada can reap the rewards of the AI boom it helped to instigate, turning technology into an economy, without Silicon Valley's help. Now they just have to prove it.

* * *

Ruslan Salakhutdinov was working at a bank in Toronto in 2005 when a chance encounter with an old professor and his math changed his trajectory. "I accidentally run into Geoff on the street, and he [says], 'Come to my office, I'll show you something really cool,'" recalls Salakhutdinov, laughing. Geoffrey Hinton had a fix for a long-standing challenge of neural networks.

Let's say you have a folder full of animal photos and you want AI to pick out the ones with cats. Coders of conventional machine-learning systems might set out features that differentiate the felines from the canines and bovines, and train their algorithms on lots of images labelled by species. Deep-learning models—named for the multiple layers of software they contain—don't need the tags. Researchers apply the system to the images themselves, leaving the system to figure out the features on which to focus.

The notion of brain-approximating machine learning has been around for decades. But for a long time, neural networks only "sort of worked, classifying things like corners of images," says Steve Woods, whose computer science doctoral studies at the University of Waterloo in the 1990s focused on conventional, search-based approaches to AI. Deep learning "just didn't scale."

Part of the problem was that training a neural net took an age on the computers of the era. The innovation Hinton demonstrated to

Salakhutdinov on that day in 2005 was to do it one layer of the network at a time, a more efficient method. "He showed me some of the mathematical formulations underlying these models," says Salakhutdinov. "And then I got sold." Instead of rising through the ranks of the banking industry, Salakhutdinov returned to U of T to get his PhD in deep learning.

Outside, a neural-net winter had set in. Canadian AI luminaries credit Toronto-based CIFAR, a government-backed research organization, with continuing to fund the field when no one else would. In 2004, it committed $2.5 million over five years to Hinton's plan for a new program called Neural Computation and Adaptive Perception (NCAP). It formed "a very vibrant, global network really pushing the boundaries of fundamental AI research," says Elissa Strome, now an executive director at CIFAR. U de M's Bengio was a member, as was Yann LeCun, a professor at New York University. (Bengio and LeCun would go on to share the Turing Award, computing's highest honour, with Hinton in 2019.)

Every July or August, the NCAP program brought together faculty and students working in the field for five days of summer school. In the early years, the class held fifteen or so people in a small conference room at U of T's computer science department. The professors would give tutorials on new methods and models, and the students would present their research. "In the afternoon we had coding sessions," says Salakhutdinov.

"I met so many people who now have tremendous careers in AI," says Hugo Larochelle, then a PhD student under Bengio at U de M and now principal scientist with Google DeepMind in Montreal. "Creating this network was very useful as a junior researcher." Summer school attendees included the likes of Roland Memisevic, Ilya Sutskever, and Raquel Urtasun, each of whom went on to launch a major AI company.

For all the warmth in those rooms, deep learning was not yet mainstream. Larochelle met a frosty reception from journals when he tried to publish his first paper. "The negative review was along the line, 'The ideas are interesting. But it's using neural networks, so no thank you,'" he says. The group persisted, motivated by the feeling that they were onto something.

A series of breakthroughs between the mid-2000s and 2010s—Larochelle and Salakhutdinov each co-authored key papers—thawed conditions. Running on faster graphics processing units (GPUs), deep learning began to beat conventional AI systems, starting with speech recognition. The real mainstreaming began in October 2012, when Hinton and students Sutskever and Alex Krizhevsky won that year's ImageNet photograph-categorization competition with a neural net. Their paper, "ImageNet classification with deep convolutional neural networks," has been cited more than 144,000 times.

Silicon Valley paid attention. The following March, Google acquired DNNresearch, the trio's shell startup. The search giant reportedly paid US$44 million, beating out Baidu, DeepMind, and Microsoft to hire the three. Hinton scaled back his academic commitments and started commuting to Google headquarters in Mountain View, Calif.

Plenty of deep-learning talent followed in the next few years. A slew of young researchers went to Google, either to its internal Brain team or to DeepMind, which Google acquired in January 2014. Others left for the likes of Apple and Microsoft. Salakhutdinov himself left U of T's computer science faculty in February 2016 for a tenured position at Carnegie Mellon University, and joined Apple part-time soon after. Pittsburgh just had more people working on machine learning, language and robotics. Canada missed out, says Salakhutdinov. "These are the drivers of that technology, and they're all . . . in the US."

* * *

Not everyone immediately left for the US. A crop of Canadian startups launched in the last decade with dreams of building platforms that would take the technology to more companies and consumers. But for many, their plans proved too expensive or came too early, leading to a string of exits to the titans of Silicon Valley.

For instance, Maluuba. Apple's launch of Siri in October 2011 gave many humans their first knowing encounter with artificial intelligence. The mobile assistant's early rival had Canadian provenance: developer Maluuba. The Waterloo startup quickly signed deals with handset makers Samsung, LG, and BlackBerry, and the assistant eventually leapt to smart TVs.

Maluuba's founders wanted to evolve the user-machine interface so that a conversation with an AI assistant felt like one with a human helper. Think of *Her*, suggests co-founder Kaheer Suleman. The Spike Jonze film, which debuted the year after Maluuba's app, is about a man's relationship with an AI operating system. Samantha, the OS, is the same whether she's coming from his computer or his phone. She's capable of empathy and common-sense reasoning. Romance ensues. But building *Her* in the early 2010s was only possible in fiction.

Maluuba needed expensive cloud infrastructure to test its technology. "The researchers always used to complain internally, 'We don't have GPUs,'" says then-CEO Sam Pasupalak.

AI also requires a lot of data on which to train. The startup scraped hundreds of hours of annotated audio from TED Talks to get started, according to co-founder Joshua Pantony.

And Maluuba needed money, as well. Pantony says the company found it difficult to raise capital in Canada at the time. Silicon Valley investors were interested in the technology but not its location. Pantony recalls one venture capitalist declining to do a deal after extensive due diligence, telling him, "We love your technology, but I don't want to do board meetings in the cold."

Maluuba eventually raised US$8.4 million from backers including the venture arms of GM and Samsung, according to PitchBook data. By late 2016, it had a machine-learning team of about twenty-five and a Montreal research lab working with Bengio's AI institute, Mila. Pasupalak had lined up deals with car companies to introduce the technology into their hands-free systems. It wasn't enough.

The following January, Microsoft announced it would acquire Maluuba for an undisclosed sum. The tech giant got an infusion of talent and Maluuba's researchers got access to massive cloud infrastructure and huge amounts of text data. "It made a lot of sense," says Suleman.

The cycle of startup and sale, familiar to successive generations of Canadian technology companies, played out again and again in the AI space in the following years as founders struggled to achieve their ambitions, or deliver the returns sought by their investors.

As Maluuba was exiting, another ambitious attempt to build an AI platform was entering the scene in Montreal. In August 2016, a group of researchers and tech executives including Beaudoin and Bengio founded Element AI. The goal was to do for machine learning what Oracle had done for databases, or Amazon for the cloud. "It was rooted in a commercial desire to build . . . a very important and fundamental product that would find application everywhere," Beaudoin says.

The company's machine-learning bona fides quickly brought significant press and investor attention. Element raised US$257 million in total, PitchBook data shows. The company's site boasted of hosting "the largest privately owned Canadian artificial intelligence R&D lab," and a network of top faculty advisors. Bengio positioned Element as a bid to stop the brain drain of AI talent to Big Tech.

But the company was slow to release products and generate significant sales, with revenue initially coming from one-off consulting projects. Others in Quebec's burgeoning tech ecosystem were put off by Element's large-scale recruitment of AI researchers and graduates. "It basically created inflation [and] talent shortage in the space," Louis Têtu, CEO of Quebec City-headquartered Coveo, told The Logic in late 2021. "The only purpose [to] bring together so many data scientists is to sell the workforce."

Element did ultimately sell to ServiceNow, a Santa Clara, Calif.-headquartered software firm in November 2020 for US$228 million. "We were a bit too early," says Beaudoin, noting no one has yet built Element's vision of a universal platform for AI. But he hopes the company's fate doesn't discourage Canadian entrepreneurs and researchers from dreaming big commercial dreams.

"When it unfolded, the lesson thrown around was, 'We got scammed' or 'Too much money was directed toward that thing,'" Beaudoin says. "I'm not sure. I think we should dare greatly."

* * *

"Why do I find neural nets interesting?" considers Nick Frosst. "Because I've always found them interesting. They just do stuff that you can't do in another way."

Here too, Hinton and his math had an influence. Neural networks cross the cognitive and computer sciences. Frosst, raised in the up-river Ottawa suburb of Manotick, Ontario, had gone to U of T in 2011 to study both. He took Hinton's neural-network introductory course.

A couple of lectures in, the professor demonstrated how the system could be used to classify digits—a six, say. "Which is, first of all, very cool itself," says Frosst. But then Hinton showed how if you ran the neural net in reverse, "it can draw a six. And it can draw a six that nobody's seen before.'"

These days, it's Frosst's neural-network creations that are interesting people—and businesses and investors. He's a co-founder of Cohere, the Toronto-headquartered startup that has fast become one of the country's most prominent AI champions. Clients integrate the firm's large language models into their products to generate text, summarize documents, and improve search.

Cohere's path runs through Canada's record of AI research prowess. After university, Frosst spent some time at Google in Waterloo, engineering neural networks for ad prediction tools. Then a researcher gig opened up at his old professor's Toronto lab. "Geoff called me: 'I want two machine-learning geniuses who are also good software engineers,'" recalls Woods, then Google's senior director of engineering for Canada.

Frosst answered the call. At Google Brain, he met Aidan Gomez. During an internship at the firm's San Francisco outpost, Gomez had been on the team that came up with the transformer, a new kind of model that considered words in context rather than one by one. Their June 2017 paper, "Attention is all you need," has been cited more than 98,000 times.

The transformer has gone on to transform the commercialization trajectory of AI, enabling the current boom in generative tools such as ChatGPT. But the takeover took time. By mid-2019, Gomez was seeing plenty of applications within Google, but "the tech just wasn't popping up everywhere like I expected."

So Frosst, Gomez, and co-founder Ivan Zhang struck out on their own with Cohere. In machine-learning terms, language is "general purpose," says Frosst. Developers can construct a single, mega-model based on it, and set it to all kinds of tasks, like summarizing news articles or reading receipts. But a large language model requires huge amounts of data and "compute," the sector shorthand for processing power. "They're so hard to make, it's really useful for a small number of companies to set out to try to make the best one they can."

It's not that small a number anymore. Over 1,100 privately held generative AI companies have raised a combined US$45 billion since the start of 2020. Cohere's cohort at the top end of the LLM market includes OpenAI, where Sutskever is chief scientist, and its San Francisco neighbours, Adept and Anthropic.

Unlike earlier Canadian AI startups, Cohere believes it can achieve its ambitions without relocating to Silicon Valley. Its founders say capital no longer cares about borders and, anyway, there's plenty of capital here.

Cohere has raised US$440 million to date. Toronto's Radical Ventures wrote the startup's first cheque. Steve Woods, now a partner at Montreal-based Inovia Capital, led Cohere's US$270-million Series C in June. "We were very interested in what was going to form around them," he says, citing opportunities to roll out Cohere's technology to Inovia's portfolio firms.

Cohere is as global as any technology company today, with offices in London and San Francisco, but all three of its co-founders are Canadian. "We like it, and we want to stay," Frosst says. "It turns out that Toronto is a pretty fucking great place to start an AI company." He appreciates the ability to work with researchers at the city's Vector Institute, and the stream of machine-learning engineers coming out of local universities.

A few blocks away from Cohere, scale-up Ada has also benefited from the country's AI scene. Both companies work with name-brand clients around the world. "I don't think it would have happened anywhere else," says CEO and co-founder Mike Murchison. Clients use Ada's platform to automate certain customer service functions via chatbots and AI phone responses. The theories of big Toronto thinkers like Hinton and Marshall McLuhan shaped how Murchison and his firm approach human-machine interactions. He also credits programs like the Creative Destruction Lab— an accelerator at the University of Toronto's business school—with helping commercialize AI research. The twenty-four firms in Ada's cohort in the program have raised US$1.02 billion among them, according to PitchBook, although the three unicorns in the class account for three-quarters of the sum.

Louis Têtu's Coveo, which makes search and recommendation tools, recently launched its own generative AI offering. "A lot of things that you hear out there have not quite found a way to monetization, and frankly immediate deployment or practical application," he said on a May earnings call. "We're the opposite." Têtu, too, intends to develop his business without leaving the country.

* * *

Scientists who once attended Hinton's NCAP summer school are now taking ideas developed there to the real world, applying machine learning to such fields as drug discovery, climate science, and beyond. In June 2021, Raquel Urtasun founded Toronto-based Waabi to raise deep learning's role in autonomous vehicles from that of bit player. Her stated goal is to "bring modern AI to self-driving."

More researchers are keen to commercialize their work, says Strome, who manages CIFAR's central role in the federal government's $568.8-million

Pan-Canadian AI Strategy. Since 2017, the program has helped subsidize universities to recruit or retain more than 120 research chairs who are teaching new cohorts of Canadian AI workers. Strome says CIFAR has seen an increase in the number of researchers working with and starting companies of late.

Some 700 private Canadian AI companies have raised a combined US$7.61 billion since the start of 2020. Funds raised in 2023 had already exceeded the previous year by November, according to PitchBook data.

Sector specialists in the venture community say the technology's transformative potential is enormous, but acknowledge some investors will get burned. With the advent of LLMs, "there are examples where, in a weekend, you could build an application which is staggeringly impressive," says Woods of Inovia Capital. "But our view has changed a little lately, back to the traditional." Startups that create valuable solutions to tangible problems and keep adapting will do well, he says.

Since selling to Microsoft, Maluuba's co-founders have been working on their own valuable solutions to tangible problems. Joshua Pantony launched a new machine-learning firm, Boosted.ai. Using financially savvy LLMs, the Toronto company sifts through reams of data to summarize important trends for portfolio managers. The firm claims 190 clients, including leading banks and hedge funds. Pantony says he sought out "the biggest possible addressable market" with "a very obvious problem [where] technology is a solution." In finance and AI, he thinks he's found a good bet.

Pantony's former partners, Sam Pasupalak and Kaheer Suleman, are working on a startup of their own. While it's still in stealth mode, both say the main product won't be AI. "It's very commoditized right now," says Pasupalak, who predicts that few firms now launching to sell applications built on top of others' LLMs will make it big. "I want to build a real company with real users, solving a real market problem."

Corporate Canada is increasingly alive to the real-world applications of AI. Foteini Agrafioti has seen the before and after. In September 2016, RBC launched Borealis AI, a lab that conducts research and builds products with the technology. "We recognized that the bank had a role to play in creating jobs for all of these great scientists that were graduating our schools [and] leaving the country," says Agrafioti, who heads the unit. The lab has since produced numerous research papers and some commercial applications, too.

In October 2020, RBC's capital-markets arm launched Aiden, an auto-trading platform. It employs reinforcement learning, an approach that DeepMind famously used to beat one of the world's best human Go players. "We knew that science was good for gaming applications," says Agrafioti, noting that a financial market is a game of sorts. The world's best human experts in reinforcement learning are at the University of Alberta, the academic home of field pioneer Rich Sutton. Borealis brought some on board and sent staff back and forth from Toronto to Edmonton to learn.

It worked. "Today, we send a lot of our trading flow through this platform," says Agrafioti.

In the world of bricks and mortar, construction giant EllisDon has used AI to improve cost and timeline projections, working off truckloads of data from hundreds of projects. The Mississauga, Ont.-based firm has piloted technology from startups, like a system that uses computer vision to capture time lapses of a building site, then compares it to the contractor's models.

EllisDon is also working with the Vector Institute to add AI tools to its project-management application, although the firm declined to disclose what those tools will do. "Clients are not asking specifically for AI," says Brandon Milner, senior vice-president of digital and data engineering. But where it can be useful, he says, the company now has the technical chops to apply it. "It's really a proactive approach."

Other executives see opportunity for AI in sustainability. "I believe in technology being useful to solve important societal problems, and I also want Montreal and Canada to have a voice in that," says Hugo Larochelle. In November 2016, he returned to the city to lead a new Google Brain unit there. He was recruited by Samy Bengio, brother of Yoshua Bengio, his former U de M professor.

One researcher on Larochelle's team worked on Project Sunroof, a tool to encourage homeowners to install solar panels by estimating how much they'd save. Others are working on a bioacoustics system designed to identify birds from song, keeping an ear on population numbers to aid conservation. "I'm hopeful that [sustainability] becomes a thriving area in AI," says Larochelle.

Philippe Beaudoin sees an opportunity to use AI to help Canada break out of its reliance on business-to-business, software-as-a-service products. The world's biggest tech companies make things for people, he says, so the country needs more founders and funders pursuing consumer AI applications. He launched Waverly in 2020 to build a social platform using "human-first" algorithms.

* * *

Billie Joe Armstrong, Harry Styles, and Gerard Way have all taken the stage at the Garage, a north London music venue of some indie notoriety. At the end of September, Nick Frosst joined that list of iconic frontmen.

The Cohere co-founder is also the singer of Good Kid, a rockish band with a wholesome vibe that is composed of five coders. "I don't use our models to generate lyrics," Frosst says, answering a question he gets asked a lot. "What I want out of art and artistry and lyric writing is self-expression." Speeding up the creative process isn't the point.

But of late, Frosst has begun using Cohere's models as a sounding board, inputting his lyrics and asking the system to say what they mean. "I use that sometimes to figure out, 'Is the metaphor or the imagery I'm using too subtle? Or am I banging it over the head?'"

Allow me one of those banging-over-the-head metaphors. Cohere could be to AI today what Nortel or BlackBerry were, respectively, to networking and smartphones when those companies were in their primes—Canada's champion in a strategic and lucrative technology sector.

Frosst resists the comparison, and not only because both Nortel and Blackberry rose to great heights and fell hard. He thinks the future may be different in this generation of technology, with many champions instead of one—"there are other excellent Canadian AI companies." Besides, his firm has ambitions to be bigger than Nortel or Blackberry ever were.

The notion of being the first name that comes to mind when people think of a successful Canadian AI company nevertheless holds appeal to Frosst. "That would be very meaningful to me," he says. "In a few years, I think we can deliver on that promise. But we still have a lot of work ahead of us."

Cohere is not alone. There is work to be across the entire Canadian AI landscape. The country will need to figure out how to keep more of its AI talent and luminaries, get the technology into more firms and sectors, continuously replenish its stock of startups as the successful ones reach scale, and ensure the rest of the population isn't left behind.

So far, we're doing fine—better than fine for a small country with middling geopolitical and economic clout. Brilliant new companies are emerging. CIFAR is still running its summer school—in July 2023, more than 150 AI students attended. The federal government has pledged hundreds of millions in funding via its national strategy and financing for individual firms. But as powerful nations and firms compete for AI leadership, Canada needs more than past research glories and aspirations of prosperity to make the most of this AI moment.

CHAPTER THREE

ROUSING CORPORATE CANADA

By Jesse Snyder

When the release of ChatGPT kicked off an artificial intelligence craze, Shelby Austin, the CEO of Toronto-based Arteria AI, received a flood of calls from international executives seeking advice on how they could get ahead of the curve on the nascent technology.

Showing notably less interest were CEOs of Canadian firms that, despite operating in some of the same markets as Arteria partners Citigroup and Goldman Sachs, appeared to have less curiosity about what the rapid advancement of large language models and other AI technologies meant for their businesses.

Austin's experience echoes macro-level findings that suggest Canada is lagging its peers when it comes to AI adoption. Some industry insiders see low AI take-up as part of a deeper risk aversion within the Canadian private sector, one that threatens to put the country at a disadvantage during a moment of rapid advancement in artificial intelligence.

The Dais, a Toronto Metropolitan University think tank, released a study in September 2023 that found only 4.7 percent of Canadian companies with ten or more employees had integrated AI into their businesses in any capacity as of 2021. The problem underscores "a trend that has been plaguing Canada for a long time," says study author Angus Lockhart.

Canada's slow AI adoption comes at a time when the technology looks poised to disrupt entire industries, potentially carrying wider implications for the country's competitive position relative to other nations. Austin, like others interviewed by the Logic, said Canadian firms tend to wait

31

until technologies are proven before investing in them. "There's just not the same demand and hunger to be leading edge," she says. "At a corporate level, there's a much more conservative ethos and reluctance to go further or be an early adopter in the space, which we think can be challenging." She gives Canada a grade of "C" for its response to the technology.

Arteria offers an AI-driven platform that financial companies use for contracting purposes. By sorting through reams of otherwise hard-to-organize data, the technology provides companies with sharper information that can assist with a range of tasks from client onboarding to loan processing, Austin says.

Jas Jaaj, managing partner for AI and data at consulting firm Deloitte, says Canada's record on AI adoption is mixed, depending on the sector. In research, financial services, and telecoms, Canada is in many respects leading the way, he says, while it trails in such sectors as construction and real estate. In academia, the number of AI-related patents generated in Canada leapt 57 percent in fiscal 2023, the second-fastest of any country.

Deloitte estimates that 26 percent of Canadian companies have adopted AI technology, a higher percentage than Dias reported, but that's lower than the global mark of 34 percent. "Corporate Canada is already falling behind its global peers" in using the technology, according to Deloitte. Actually implementing AI technologies at commercial scale will require considerably more thought and investment. "The leap that we have to take now is to take these prototypes and then deploy them into production and scale them across the enterprise," says Jaaj.

Sheldon Fernandez, CEO of Waterloo's DarwinAI, said there is a marked difference in the approach to technological adoption between Canadian and US firms. His company sells a microwave-sized device that uses AI to scan for potential faults on printed circuit boards, automating a visual factory-floor inspection process that was previously done by humans.

Roughly half of DarwinAI's dozen clients are Canadian, but Fernandez said US and other foreign firms tend to have a higher appetite for risk and investing in new technologies like AI. "In general, Canadian companies are a lot more risk averse than their American counterparts," he says.

When DarwinAI launched a separate product during the pandemic, a platform that monitored AI programs and offered insights into how they ultimately came to decisions, just one of the company's ten clients was Canadian. "I used to lament that here we have cutting-edge IP invented by a Canadian company, connected to the University of Waterloo, doing wonderful things," he says. "And the companies that were benefiting from this were all American corporations."

Nevertheless, Fernandez and others say there are signs Canadian companies might be improving their uptake. Canadian firms, including Shopify, Coveo Solutions, and many others, have embraced generative AI technology as a way to drive down costs, automate customer services, and improve countless other aspects of their businesses.

Deloitte's Jaaj points out that the technology has the potential to help companies improve operations and develop new products at a fraction of previous costs. "This trend with generative AI is going to help us because you can now subscribe to a service from these large language model providers—be it through Microsoft, be it through Google, etc.—to be able to use their APIs, their interfaces, and be able to build solutions by tapping into the models that they have trained."

Sam Ramadori, CEO of Montreal-based Brainbox AI, says a major hindrance among would-be AI adopters is a lack of consistent data to feed into software systems. Data is often siloed between various divisions within a company, he says, or stored in inconsistent formats or with different naming conventions. Adopting AI often entails the tedious task of streamlining those disparate data pools.

"You have that layer that you have to go and solve . . . before getting to the benefits of AI," he says. "There is a bit of a leap there."

Brainbox sells an AI-driven software system that monitors and adjusts heating and cooling functions in commercial buildings. The system ingests information on a room-to-room basis from a building's furnaces, thermostats, moisture sensors, and other applications, then uses AI to make constant adjustments aimed at lowering heating costs and increasing efficiency. Brainbox has installed the technology in over 1,000 commercial buildings, including the big-box stores of mattress maker Sleep Country.

While many of the company's clients are Canadian, Ramadori agrees that Canadian companies tend to be more hesitant to adopt the technology. He sees the problem as broader than AI, attributing it to the risk aversion permeating industries across the country. "It's an unfortunate, recognized state of affairs: that in Canada, we're just generally more conservative and slower to adopt new technology."

Tardier uptake is likely to have broader implications for Canada's private sector as AI is integrated throughout the global economy. Artificial intelligence, says Austin of Arteria AI, is "undeniable." It is set to become a dominant technology in coming years, regardless of whether Canadian companies choose to join the fray. "And as a result, if you're not using it, and everyone else has it as a tool in their toolbox, it begs the question: where are you going to be in one year, two years, five years?"

CHAPTER FOUR

LABOUR'S RED LINE

By Martin Patriquin

As supervisor of what he calls the "boots-on-the-ground squad," Luca Mascetti oversees the upkeep of McGill University's more than 100 buildings, along with the thirty-two-hectare downtown campus where they sit. The job is a farrago of work orders, equipment breakdowns, shift schedules, and constant uncertainty as to what Mother Nature has in store. Mascetti loves the work, and he also loves that his job is the most secure against the job-disrupting, AI-assisted tide barreling toward us.

Only one percent of groundskeeping and maintenance workers are exposed to automation by AI, according to a recent Goldman Sachs report. That's good news to the nearly 327,000 such employees Statistics Canada reports are working in the country, Mascetti and his crew included. The least secure, according to Goldman Sachs, are Canada's roughly 164,000 office and administrative support workers, nearly half of whom will see AI disrupt their jobs, if it doesn't eliminate them altogether.

Organized labour is becoming a powerful voice on anxieties surrounding AI adoption in the workplace and a potentially formidable bulwark against the spread of the technology.

FTQ, the union federation representing the groundskeepers and other employees at McGill, says AI has the potential "to attack certain fundamental rights." The Canadian Union of Public Employees (CUPE) says "the rapid emergence of artificial intelligence . . . represents a growing and evolving threat to many of our fields of work." The union, the county's largest, has pledged to protect the livelihood of its 740,000 members "where AI and technology threatens jobs and livelihoods."

35

In September, the Alliance of Canadian Cinema Television and Radio Artists (ACTRA) said AI poses an "existential threat" to the industry. The union, which represents 28,000 performers across the country, negotiated some protections for its members in the video-game industry. The Screen Actors Guild-American Federation of Television and Radio Artists (SAG-AFTRA) ended a nearly four-month strike in November 2023 after securing a contract with Hollywood studios that, among other things, promised "lengthy and detailed AI guardrails."

Canadian workers are among the faster adopters of AI in the world, according to a 2023 LinkedIn Future of Work Report. Yet language like CUPE'S has some worried that organized labour will stifle Canada's technological future. "Fear" is the biggest hindrance to AI adoption in the Canadian workplace, says Nicole Janssen, co-CEO of the Edmonton-based AI solutions company AltaML. "Unions and organized labour getting behind that messaging is just going to keep it around."

Nearly 30 percent of Canadian jobs are unionized, which leaves potential for a lot of pushback. And employees are only starting to grasp how AI might affect their careers. In a PwC survey of Canadian workers published in July 2023, less than half of respondents had a good sense of how the skills their jobs require will change in the next few years, and nearly a third said they doubted artificial intelligence will have an impact on their jobs. Many may be underestimating the impact of the technology, the authors concluded.

A closer look, however, reminds us that the workforce—including the part made up of unionized employees—is not a monolith. A sizable chunk of the labour movement has embraced the work-enhancing benefits of the technology and seeks only to curb its potentially exploitative effects on its members. In 2018, Unifor, the country's largest private-sector union, produced a report addressing for the first time how it would approach the use of AI. While it outlined the technology's potential pitfalls for workers, including job losses and increased surveillance, the report was candid about AI's inevitability and its potential upsides:

Reading the headlines, one cannot be blamed for thinking that artificial intelligence is going to take over the world—imminently. However, the general consensus among researchers and AI experts suggests that humans are far more likely to be working alongside machines during their future work than being entirely replaced, though what one's job looks like could change dramatically in the process.

Five years later, Unifor's view is largely unchanged. With AI, "there will be tasks that will be replaced more than whole jobs," says Kaylie Tiessen, a research analyst with the union. "What we need to do as workers is mitigate the risks and seize the opportunity, recognizing that there are opportunities to potentially make jobs higher quality. But that requires transparency between workers and employers with lots of consultation and discussion on technological change."

Surveillance counts among Tiessen's chief concerns. While remote tracking of employee activity existed before COVID-19 triggered a mass departure from offices, the use of AI has only increased the practice, particularly in the trucking industry, says Tiessen.

The worry is that employers will use AI-derived data to discipline workers, something Amazon has already done with its drivers. Another very real and perhaps more insidious concern is that employers will use the data gathered through surveillance systems to automate certain jobs out of existence. "There are programs that are constantly listening to you and watching you to provide advice on how a customer service agent should be interacting with a customer. At the same time, you may be training an AI that is going to eventually replace you," says Tiessen.

Still others worry about AI's potentially destructive effects on the social safety net should the technology be used to replace human decisions. In 2021, the Quebec government launched a five-year strategy to integrate AI into the province's public sector. Government Administration Minister Sonia LeBel says AI has "invaluable potential to public administration." Not everyone is convinced.

"One of the things that preoccupies us the most is in welfare," says Isaïe-Nicolas Dubois-Sénéchal, a researcher with the SFPQ, which represents public and parapublic service workers in Quebec. Dubois-Sénéchal says many frontline SFPQ members will be trained to use an "algorithm system" for social assistance applicants. He worries AI will eventually usurp his members' decision-making power. "This involves people with extremely complex cases which are extremely varied. So to have this managed by artificial intelligence is something that is excessively dangerous for us."

There is much at stake. Generative AI alone could raise labour productivity by 0.1 to 0.6 percent annually until 2040, according to a recent McKinsey report. While some experts worry about the slow rate of AI adoption by Canadian corporations, labour sees it being used at an alarming rate to streamline existing systems and open new data streams. Canadian Tire is employing AI to help determine store layouts and stocking models. The company has also experimented at its Mark's and Sport Chek stores with an AI-powered robot that can learn rudimentary tasks like tagging products and folding clothes. During the pandemic, grocery store giant Loblaws hoovered up AI experts and data technicians in anticipation of the transition to come.

Whether those projects succeed hangs on any number of variables, from the design of the technology to companies' tolerance for failure. But the greatest hurdle, says Janssen, may be overcoming workers' collective worry. "Somewhere between 20 and 30 percent of AI models built actually get implemented," she says. "There's a lot of factors to adoption, and why that happens. But probably the biggest is fear."

CHAPTER FIVE

BRAIN DRAIN

By Catherine McIntyre & Leah Golob

Deon Nicholas was in high school when he was initiated into Canada's emerging AI industry. It started with back-to-back summer internships at the renowned Alberta Machine Intelligence Institute (Amii). There, Nicholas worked alongside some of the world's greatest AI thinkers, including Richard Sutton, known as the godfather of reinforcement learning, whose research was yet another important Canadian contribution to technologies such as ChatGPT.

Nicholas had barely known what AI was before that first internship in 2010. He became hooked on machine learning and went on to study computer science and math at the University of Waterloo. He worked on AI projects off the side of his desk. He took online courses outside the university on natural language processing and co-authored an academic paper with researchers back at Amii.

When it came time to start his own company, Nicholas opted to launch in San Francisco despite his early exposure to Canada's AI pipeline. "I didn't actually think about going anywhere else," he says.

As the co-founder and CEO of venture-backed generative AI startup Forethought, Nicholas is yet another example of a young talent schooled at one of the country's three AI institutes—Amii in Edmonton, the Vector Institute in Toronto, and Mila in Montreal—only to be lost to the Bay Area orbit of Big Tech

Canada's world-class AI researchers, including Sutton, Geoffrey Hinton, and Yoshua Bengio, have not only established the country as a global leader in the sector but developed a hotbed of talent along the way. Over 4,000 people enrolled in or graduated from Canadian AI programs in 2022–23, according to a recent Deloitte Canada report. Canada ranked first among G7 nations in the number of AI research publications per capita that same year. "Of the world's most elite AI researchers (i.e., the top 0.5 percent)," the report reads, "six percent call Canada home."

In the year following the launch of ChatGPT, competition for Canadian talent became fierce. Job postings on LinkedIn that mentioned AI or generative AI more than doubled globally between July 2021 and July 2023. Big Tech companies are offering hundreds of thousands of dollars to fill AI engineer jobs, while a product manager at Netflix could earn up to US$900,000 a year. Amazon announced plans to train two million people globally by 2025 through its "AI Ready" program after an AWS survey found that while 73 percent of employers said hiring AI workers was a priority, almost three-quarters of those employers said they can't find the AI talent they need.

As more companies, investors, and governments outside Canada funnel massive resources into the sector, the country is at more risk than ever of losing its homegrown talent. "A lot of US companies are really willing to invest and go hard in the area," says Amii CEO Cam Linke. "A lot of that talent that wants to build big, interesting things is evaluating whether or not Canada is the place that they can do that."

* * *

Brain drain is not unique to Canada's AI sector. The country's robust research institutions have long generated large talent pools in STEM (science, technology, engineering, and mathematics) fields. After earning an education and research experience in Canada, some of that talent inevitably moves south where there tends to be a greater abundance of high-paying jobs. The dynamic often leaves Canadian companies scrambling for the talent trained by the country's universities.

But the consequences for Canada of losing its AI talent are potentially more severe than with other industries, not least because AI promises to transform virtually every aspect of the economy and society. "If we are not attracting talent, developing talent, our companies are not going to be able to be good adopters of this technology," says Salim Teja, a partner at Toronto's Radical Ventures. "And our innovators are not going to have access to the talent that they need."

Nicholas says he was drawn to Silicon Valley after working there in two co-op placements as an undergraduate student, one with Facebook, the other with data-analytics giant Palantir. The prestige of those firms and the generous wages on offer made them hard for Nicholas to resist. When he began thinking of starting his own company, San Francisco was an obvious choice. He had already established a peer network. "One of the things I found about the Bay Area was that the network, that connectivity, and the culture of people starting companies, is unparalleled," he says.

Since launching Forethought in 2018, Nicholas has recruited other Canadians to work for him. The company, which uses generative AI for customer service, has hired University of Waterloo co-op students and graduates, sponsoring visas to relocate some of them to the US. It also has a partnership with Amii to collaborate on research and access talent to help fill jobs at Forethought.

Nicholas says he's also keen to hire more remote workers based in Canada. Doing so allows him to pay lower salaries than typical in Silicon Valley, and he hopes it will help him qualify for Canada's flagship research incentive, the scientific research and economic development tax credit.

As Nicholas learned as an undergrad, salaries are significantly lower in Canada. Chris Welsh, founder and partner at the Toronto staffing and recruiting firm People Machine, told The Logic that companies can hire two employees in Toronto for the price of one in Silicon Valley, adjusting for the exchange rate. That makes it difficult for Canadian firms to compete.

Some companies fight back by emphasizing that there is more to work than earning a handsome salary. They emphasize their exciting new technologies and the chance to do work with a higher purpose. There are growing opportunities in AI aimed at tackling issues related to climate change and the health-care industry, Welsh says. People want to "feel like they're making society better, as opposed to just selling more product."

At Toronto-based Promise Robotics, many applicants are drawn to the company's mission to help solve the housing and climate crises, according to co-founder and CEO Ramtin Attar. The two-year-old software company uses AI to train robots to build energy-efficient houses through processes that cut back on material waste. Since raising close to $21 million in October 2023, Promise has had a flood of job applications. But the company, which grew its workforce by 200 percent between May and December 2023, has found recruiting for senior AI experts challenging.

"Either, as a startup, you cannot afford it in the early days," says Attar, "or they're just more comfortable on the research side." The excitement that ChatGPT has created around large language models is another obstacle for Promise, he adds, with some applicants dropping out of the hiring process in favour of jobs that focus on LLMs.

* * *

Canada has tried to get ahead in the AI talent wars. In 2017, Ottawa launched the Pan-Canadian AI Strategy, a core focus of which was to attract, train, and retain AI talent. The federal government selected the Canadian Institute for Advanced Research (CIFAR) to lead the talent part of the strategy, arming the think tank with over $200 million for the initiative. CIFAR's strategy centres on appointing research chairs to Canada's three AI institutes. It has sponsored 122 chairs since 2018 and, in 2023 alone, 254 students supervised by those chairs graduated from master's, PhD, or postdoctoral programs.

While generous salaries and prestigious work lure some of this talent to the US tech giants, there are indications that the volume of talent staying at home has been increasing. According to Deloitte Canada's recent AI report, the vast majority—about 92 percent since 2018—of AI master's program graduates affiliated with the Vector Institute in Toronto stay in Ontario after graduation.

Canada's big banks are helping out by relying on talent from Canadian academic institutions and research organizations when recruiting. Foteini Agrafioti, head of RBC's research centre, Borealis AI, says the centre understands the "value, thought leadership, and information" they bring and is focused on strengthening relationships with CIFAR and the Vector Institute, as well as other accelerators and organizations in the Canadian AI ecosystem. Similarly, National Bank has established numerous partnerships with universities and research centres such as the Montreal-based Institute for Data Valorization to attract AI expertise.

But Salim Teja, whose Radical Ventures backs some of Canada's most promising AI startups, warns against getting comfortable. "The danger we have is, if we all feel like our mission is done, we'll lose our stature globally," he says, "because other regions and other countries around the world are equally as focused on ramping up their talent-development initiatives."

It would also be a mistake to read too much into Deloitte's high retention rates. They don't necessarily mean these AI employees are with Canadian firms. The rise of remote work has created opportunities for Canadians to take US jobs without relocating. Meta, Samsung, Unity Technologies, and HCL Technologies are among the companies taking advantage of local talent. In November 2023, Unilever launched its global AI lab in Toronto. The London-based consumer-goods giant said in a press release that it chose the city because of its "concentration of AI expertise."

Notwithstanding the banks, Canadian companies' cautious adoption of AI technology doesn't bode well for local talent, says Teja. "If we're creating a talent engine, and then there's no receptors for all of the talent that we're trying to scale, they're going to go elsewhere."

That could change as Canada's AI ecosystem matures, opening the door to bigger opportunities and salaries that better compete with global firms. A growing cohort of AI startups and scale-ups in Canada could serve as landing pads for talent coming out of the country's research institutions. Attar says Promise, for instance, has hired exclusively from Canada's talent pool.

Nevertheless, says Linke, if Canada is serious about keeping its AI lead, policymakers need to be far more ambitious. "If we really want to win at the talent piece, if we want to win in this overall, we need to stop thinking about [being] 10 percent better." Rather, Canada should aim to increase AI jobs and the talent to fill them tenfold, he says. "That's how we get to global scale and global impact."

CHAPTER SIX

A BUG'S MOONSHOT

By Anita Balakrishnan

The world's top experts on the ant, that humblest of insects, are conservatively outnumbered about 20 quadrillion to one by their research subjects. There are 15,700 named ant species and subspecies, and potentially just as many undiscovered. Never mind studying all that variety, keeping track of it is a job that stretches the limits of human capability—particularly in a world changing so rapidly that an estimated 1 million animal and plant species are threatened with extinction, the most in human history.

Bug scientists are hoping artificial intelligence can help solve the mysteries of the natural world scurrying beneath our feet and protect biodiversity. Biologist John Fryxell is leading one such effort.

In a sleepy building at the University of Guelph about 100 kilometres west of Toronto, Fryxell's team is hatching an AI program designed to bust through a bottleneck in a process its research describes as "intensive, laborious, and prohibitively expensive."

"There is essentially nobody on the face of the planet that's capable of sitting down and identifying every single specimen [of bug] that could be brought in, based on their knowledge. That's beyond human capacity," says Fryxell.

Scientists have been working over the past few decades to collect vast numbers of specimens in a comprehensive way, he says, but "that hasn't been accompanied with armies of people to try and identify those specimens. We need to find other ways to achieve that—one is through deep learning."

Fryxell and other researchers are working on a project called BugShot, which uses deep learning, high-definition cameras, and computer vision to help identify bugs from bulk samples of preserved insect carcasses that would normally have to be sorted by hand—potentially cutting the process down from about a year to an hour or two. BugShot can classify over 1,000 arthropods—those are bugs with exoskeletons, from spiders to millipedes—into groupings and estimate the biomass from a single photo, Fryxell and other researchers wrote in a paper in *Methods in Ecology and Evolution*.

AI has its limits, at least for now. The system focuses on identifying and grouping broad categories. While identifying bugs down to the species level would be the "gold standard," they are still at the early stages of developing methods to get that granular, Fryxell says. Humans have to lend the system a helping hand.

One recent fall morning, co-op student Andrea Kolodziej was doing just that, readying a sample from Sweden under a rig with white screens and ring lights that looks like it belongs to a TikTok influencer, but smells like 90 percent ethanol. Holding up a large, spider-esque creature, Kolodziej picked out the many smaller bugs entombed in its grasp that might otherwise be missed by AI. Research technician Nao Ito noted that humans must ensure the computer doesn't match legs to the wrong torsos.

"From a machine-learning standpoint, the problems are actually really challenging. It's not just, 'Oh, apply this off-the-shelf stuff,'" says Graham Taylor, a University of Guelph engineering professor and member of the Vector Institute for Artificial Intelligence. He's been putting the call out for more computer scientists to pursue the project, which is both technically challenging and furthers the "more meaningful" cause of preserving biodiversity. "It really scares me that you can take a walk and hearing all those noises that you hear in the background when you're in the forest could just disappear."

The technology is a leap toward a dream of bug scientists, who since the 1990s have been working on computer vision to train AI in extracting meaning from insect images, the same way that a scientist would. Other methods required building different algorithms for different types of bugs, or were limited to classifying a single arthropod per image, or needed human annotations.

Amid hand wringing about how Canada can best take advantage of AI's hot moment, BugShot combines two of the country's powerhouse projects: the Vector Institute's AI prowess and the University of Guelph's massive repository of biodiversity data—including its library of bug shots. Two decades ago, University of Guelph scientists pioneered an identification system for potentially every organism in the world called DNA bar-coding; the university's BOLD database has more than 10 million specimen records, 3.5 million specimen images, and more than a million users globally. It was a breakthrough that put Canada's biologists on the map, opening opportunities for collaboration on other projects like BugShot.

Otso Ovaskainen, a research director of the organismal and evolutionary biology program at the University of Helsinki, says Guelph's status as a biodiversity hub, plus the presence of AI experts like Taylor, helped attract him to the program. Fryxell's Guelph lab is working with Ovaskainen on a project called Lifeplan, a worldwide effort to "generate the most ambitious, globally distributed, and systematically collected dataset to date" in a bid to catalog biodiversity before it disappears.

"There is a lot of excitement about AI in biodiversity research," says Ovaskainen. "Now, it's really possible to do a comprehensive, systematic, calibrated sampling of the world's biodiversity . . . which was simply not possible, let's say ten years ago."

Fryxell, whose lab conducts research projects as far-flung as the Serengeti or Norway's Boreal reindeer habitats, says insects can play "a very large economic role" in society as well. Experts are overwhelmed not only with collecting and cataloguing the presence and prevalence of the world's bugs in different habitats—they're staving off what the Bugshot research paper calls "the potential threat of food web collapse."

Activist campaigns to "save the bees" have raised awareness of how humans depend on insects for a massive share of the world's crop pollination, a service that, according to one estimate, is worth US$577 billion to the global economy. Reports of a potential "insect apocalypse" document how some fish are getting smaller and some European farmland birds are starving because their insect food source is declining. Major companies like Bayer have started working with scientists to measure how insect populations are impacted by their pesticides.

Fryxell says that while we might view some bugs as nuisances, there are many that do important jobs such as pollinate food or help control the populations of worse pests. "We all know about the importance of pollinators and making sure that our plant crops are appropriately fertilized and grow each year. A lot of our food production, for example, relies on these insect collaborators to basically do that job [of pollination] for us," he says. "We often . . . have very little awareness of this armada of insect helpers."

Amid all the warnings about AI's destructive potential, Bugshot is an example of how its growing power can help solve massive problems facing humanity and the planet. "It's difficult to imagine anything that would be very negative in this particular application," says Fryxell. "It helps emphasize that AI is not a completely negative, maligned force in the world."

CHAPTER SEVEN

DRUG DISCOVERY

By David Reevely & Aleksandra Sagan

The sidewalks around AbCellera's main Vancouver office were closed at times during the summer of 2023, due to local construction. Its hundreds of employees found it difficult to access the five-storey headquarters they have already outgrown. Soon, much of the company's staff will move into new, custom-built space one street away, filling an additional 380,000 square feet across two buildings. The urgent expansion of AbCellera's campus reflects the company's emergence as a leader in finding new ways to fight disease via antibody therapies its scientists discover with the help of artificial intelligence.

The pharmaceutical research sector offers some of the best examples of domestic companies trying to build on the opportunities created by the vital early AI breakthroughs that were made in Canada's research universities and laboratories. It also offers some of the clearest examples of the challenges companies face in this market as they try to scale up and compete on the global stage.

With a record-breaking IPO in its rearview mirror, AbCellera is often lauded as a success story. It's an exception. While Canada has gained renown for its prowess in the first stages of AI-assisted pharmaceutical research, biotech leaders say they need more of many things if the country wants to turn its early lead in AI drug discovery into more AbCelleras. More wet labs, where they can perform tests in real-world conditions they've previously modelled on computers. More manufacturing space to make the products they develop. More financial investment. And, according to some in the increasingly competitive field, a bit more can-do spirit.

CEO Carl Hansen remembers when AbCellera existed in a University of British Columbia lab with a half-dozen employees and modest ambitions that saw them leave a local pitch competition dejected.

Hansen and the others, following a piece of bad advice they'd received while preparing for the competition, included an exit plan in their pitch. They set their sights on being acquired for $100 million within eight years. Their pitch was met with incredulity. "It can't be done. It's too big," he recalls being told. AbCellera's first day of trading, roughly eight years after it was founded, gave it a market capitalization of nearly US$16 billion.

That propensity to think small—distinctly Canadian, in Hansen's estimation—is a big part of why Canadian startups fail to scale into global powerhouses. To him, AbCellera's status as a Vancouver anchor firm is an insufficient marker of success. "The game in biotech or technology or business in general is not to win in your neighbourhood or in your province, or even in your country," he says. "It's to win on a global stage." In Hansen's mind, AbCellera has only just entered that arena.

On a Tuesday afternoon, sitting in one of the company's sun-drenched meeting spaces, Hansen seemed frustrated by the hype around AI in drug discovery. He pointed to a line in the company's latest annual report: "Many of the claims associated with AI drug discovery are ahead of current capabilities." In conversation, he offered a translation: "We're calling BS on a lot of this."

While some AI applications for drug discovery are powerful, "it is not a Star Trek computer. You can't go to this thing and ask it, 'Hey, can you give me an antibody drug?' That's currently science fiction."

But, then, five years ago, Philip Kim would have told you the work his University of Toronto lab does today was impossible.

He'd published on machine learning in biochemistry in 2003, practically the dawn of time in this field, when he was finishing a PhD at the Massachusetts Institute of Technology. Now a molecular biologist cross-appointed to U of T's computer-science department, he works on how proteins (and peptides, their building blocks) interact in biological systems. A peptide that interferes with certain cells could be the basis of a cancer drug. One that helps brain cells stay together could fight Parkinson's.

A monumental obstacle in Kim's field was that a computer understands a protein molecule as a long set of three-dimensional coordinates. Teaching it that if you rotate the molecule a few degrees, its new coordinates represent the same protein, is essential. Especially if you're sifting through millions of them. "All the numbers have changed, so for the computer, it's a new object," Kim says. "There are ways to counteract that, but it becomes very inefficient."

As artificial intelligence researchers knocked these barriers down, progress in AI-assisted biochemistry accelerated, to the point where it's now commercially attractive because simulations of chemicals are nearly as good for understanding their properties as the real things in test tubes. "In 2023, if you can dream up the protein on the computer, it's going to do more or less exactly what you want," says Kim.

He attributes much of the progress in his field to AI all-stars Geoffrey Hinton, one of Kim's colleagues, and Yoshua Bengio at the Université de Montréal. Neither is a biologist or a chemist, but both attracted and trained talented people to create world-class AI ecosystems in Toronto and Montreal.

In 2012, a student of Hinton's, George Dahl, led a group that won a $40,000 prize sponsored by Merck for finding statistical techniques to predict certain molecules' biological effects. That was a side hustle. Dahl's main PhD research was on using AI in speech recognition.

As rich as the Toronto ecosystem is, it is incomplete. Kim is a co-founder of a venture-backed pharma startup that remains in stealth mode, so he's circumspect about its mission, other than saying it involves designing biologic drugs. When the time comes to take potential medicines off the screen and into a wet lab for real-life experiments, "that will probably have to be in one of the US hubs, so likely Boston," he says. Toronto just doesn't have facilities and talent on anything like that scale.

Nowhere in Canada does, says Kim. A Moderna research centre in Montreal—a component of a deal the company made to build a factory there—and AbCellera's Vancouver expansion could be parts of a solution. But not many pharmaceutical firms have gone from idea to commercial product here. "There are certainly some successes, but the list is pretty short," Kim says.

AbCellera has attacked the problem by building some of the infrastructure itself. The firm partners with other companies that come to it with a hypothesis—say, that an antibody developed for one of the tens of thousands of proteins our bodies make could help treat cancer. AbCellera then creates large numbers of antibodies, looking for the select few needles in the haystack that could become drugs.

With US pharma giant Eli Lilly, AbCellera co-developed two antibody treatments for COVID-19. They started by screening more than 5.5 million immune cells and found more than 2,000 antibodies, which AbCellera whittled down to twenty-four frontrunners within about three weeks.

The company's secret sauce is end-to-end capability for drug discovery, says Steven Mah, a senior research analyst for life science and diagnostic tools at TD Cowen. They source, search out, analyze, and engineer antibodies. "They're one of the few companies that put all of the key differentiators together and brought all these technologies under one roof into a faster and more efficient workflow."

They're working on the next logical step in that chain. In June 2021, AbCellera secured a site to build a manufacturing facility in Vancouver, which the company expects to be operational in 2025. It will produce antibodies for Phase 1 clinical trials. That will help AbCellera attract partners, says Mah, because those companies won't have to find third-party firms to do their manufacturing.

* * *

What wet labs are to a scientist like Kim, growth capital is to a CEO like Naheed Kurji, the head of Recursion Canada. Until recently, he'd been chief executive of a Toronto company named Cyclica. He joined the firm in 2014 when it was still a nestling, after first hearing about it in business school.

On the same day in May 2023, both Cyclica and Montreal's Valence Discovery sold to Recursion, an AI-driven drug-development company in Utah. Cyclica and Valence both made AI tools for discovering drug candidates. Cyclica's Toronto staff merged with a small Recursion operation already in Toronto, while Valence Discovery became Valence Labs, a Recursion research centre.

"Canada is the best in the world at defining the scientific problem and doing all the brute-force, basic research to come up with the invention to solve that problem scientifically," Kurji said recently in a video interview from Recursion Canada's new office on Toronto's Queen Street West. Finding funding to go to the next level is another matter.

AbCellera has joined calls for Canada to give special tax treatment to the revenue from Canadian discoveries and inventions, so the money can be reinvested in Canadian operations. But many companies would still need outside investment to take an innovation global.

Kurji dates investor interest in AI-driven drug research to a 2013 paper from consulting firm McKinsey & Company proposing that machine learning could give new energy to languid development pipelines. "What McKinsey says, people start to pay attention to," Kurji says.

But the sector is not for skinflints. Sometimes in pharma, hundreds of millions of dollars and decades of research and development fall flat. "It's a highly esoteric space that requires a long-term view and a patient approach to investment," Kurji says. "And that's generally not the way in which Canada has built itself."

Cyclica chose early on to stay in Canada to keep ready access to the local talent, he says, but ultimately ran up against a shortage of capital for massive growth. Some US venture firms are looking north, seeing opportunity in filling the capital gap, he says, but "that next inflection is still difficult."

Selling to Recursion means Cyclica's early backers can recycle their profits into new investments and researchers can work on new discoveries, Kurji says. He also thinks it's important that Recursion is committed to a Canadian operation—the one he now heads. "We did not sell out and move our IP and talent," Kurji says.

One Canadian money man has some ambivalence about the buyouts. "Our investors are very happy with the exits," says Jean-François Pariseau, a co-founder of Montreal's Amplitude Ventures. "But is it the best way to build a national industry? I'm not sure."

Amplitude spun out of the Business Development Bank of Canada (BDC), where Pariseau and several other members of the team were venture investors, raising $200 million for its first fund. Valence Discovery was in Amplitude's portfolio until Recursion bought it.

Pariseau, who was educated as a biologist, says Amplitude seeks to invest in companies that use AI as a tool, not as an end in itself: "When companies start slapping 'AI' on their website or at their door, that is when we get a bit less interested."

He agreed with Kurji that buyouts—the Cyclica and Valence sales are just a couple of recent examples—mean talented entrepreneurs can start again and be funded again. At BDC, Pariseau's team invested in Montreal's Clementia, a unicorn that the Paris-based pharmaceutical giant Ipsen bought in 2019. Now Clementia's ex-CEO Clarissa Desjardins leads Congruence Therapeutics, another of Amplitude's portfolio companies. What's Congruence's aim? Using AI to hunt for molecules that can correct disease-causing protein defects.

"All these companies that were acquired recently, we know them very well," Pariseau says. "All the entrepreneurs that were very successful, they're still pretty young, and they're going to be repeat entrepreneurs, and we're going to work with them, and the next companies they're going to be building will be even bigger."

CHAPTER EIGHT

ON DEFENCE

By David Reevely

Since the Second World War, military thinking has been dominated by
the warships and bombers that great powers still use to exert geopolitical
might. But as a new generation of battlefield technology comes online,
Canada has begun preparing for forms of warfare that look little like those
seen in the conflicts of the last eighty years.

Ukraine has shown what cheap drones directly piloted by humans
can do in surveillance, artillery targeting, and even tank destruction with
modified grenades dropped into open hatches. The drone lessons are
readily applied by any small force fighting a bigger, better-equipped one:
Hamas has used them against Israeli troops.

Now imagine a swarm of ten drones, collectively taking broad instruc-
tions from a person but following algorithmic rules to determine how to
carry out those orders. They might not "decide" what to destroy, but they
could decide for themselves how to react if one, or five, or nine of them
are shot down on their way to the target they've been given. Devices like
these will need artificial intelligence to be maximally effective.

The concept is called "autonomous, attritable mass," says Eliot Pence,
formerly the head of international business development for Anduril,
a California-based AI-oriented defence vendor specializing in sensors,
drones, and the software to control them and analyze their data

Autonomous means pieces of hardware that can navigate and carry
out actions on their own, including changing course or even objectives
if circumstances change around them. *Attritable* means you won't be too
bothered if you lose a few. *Mass* means a whole lot of them.

"People talk about swarms of drones overwhelming jamming and radar [defences], rather than specific strike missiles that are exquisite and hit a very narrow target," Pence says. Canada has been a leader in a lot of the technology that would guide such devices.

Now a venture capitalist and chief commercial officer at California-based Cambium, which aims to sell military hardware made with novel materials (such as drones that can withstand flames), Pence is a Canadian, raised on Vancouver Island. He laments that his homeland is behind in the field. "We have produced the most AI researchers, in Montreal. We have the most AI startups, in Toronto. And the military is just sort of asleep at the wheel. It's just baffling," says Pence.

The Canadian Forces and Department of National Defence says it hasn't been asleep—just working on these matters quietly. The department has been finalizing an artificial intelligence strategy for Canada's military, says Defence Minister Bill Blair. "We recognize that artificial intelligence can enhance information analysis, speed up decision-making, and optimize resource allocation," Blair wrote to The Logic. "Moreover, AI can strengthen logistics and supply chains; intelligence and surveillance capabilities; and training and education. We must take advantage of this opportunity."

When it's finished, he went on, the strategy "will recognize the strategic imperative of AI in the military domain, and outline measures to ensure interoperability with key allies, and proceed with the responsible development and use of AI capabilities."

It has the potential to be an ambitious plan. Canada's military lags both its allies and potential adversaries in efforts to integrate AI. Analysts have warned for years that China sees AI development as an opportunity to leapfrog the advantages others hold in conventional weapons. A military force without artificial intelligence capabilities will have a hard time holding its own against one with them.

For Canada to catch up, it will take more than just pursuing techno-logical advances. It will require a basic re-thinking of what Canada buys for its armed forces and how it buys it, and clear direction on what the Canadian military is even for, says Pence.

Weapons like those Pence describes aren't even on Blair's list of potential Canadian military uses for AI technology. Canada is officially against *fully* autonomous lethal weaponry, although Pence's drone swarms wouldn't necessarily qualify as fully autonomous if humans assigned their targets. But there are plenty of other ways AI could make a difference in geopolitical and military conflicts.

At the level of strategy, war-gaming is only beginning to incorporate artificial intelligence, according to a recent roundup by researchers funded by Britain's defence research organization. "While many ideas are circulating on how AI *could* improve war-gaming workflows, few real-world case studies offer concrete evidence of effectiveness," they wrote.

Artificial intelligence is much better at quantitative work than qualitative, which means it's more useful for, say, modelling an expeditionary force's fuel needs than simulating specific humans' choices, especially in unique circumstances like an international confrontation.

Which is not to say that such efforts aren't underway. A firm called CulturePulse is working for the United Nations, creating an AI model of the people in Israel and the Palestinian territories to help predict what would happen in response to large-scale changes in things like economic prosperity or stricter security.

In the near term, however, "the greatest benefits from AI are going to be coming from logistics chains, decision-making," says Michael Smith, the chief operating officer of Ottawa's One9, a venture capital fund focused on dual-use technologies, or tech that has both military and civilian applications.

One9 is led by Canadian special-operations veteran Glenn Cowan and Shopify co-founder Daniel Weinand. Smith emphasized he does not speak for the military, but he himself is a veteran and reservist as a military lawyer who has advised on air-force targeting in operations against ISIS. "Why wouldn't you want to use predictive algorithms for vehicle maintenance or weapons maintenance?" he says.

Smith slipped into character as an AI keeping a digital eye on artillery pieces: "I know that generally over this amount of time, it's probably firing X number of rounds, so I'm going to ping the armourer that he should probably check the following serial numbers to inspect the barrels or check the bearings on the trucks."

A ChatGPT-like tool could help write orders, he says. A more sophisticated one could propose tactical plans. An algorithm could scour social media feeds hunting for intelligence on a particular person, or "watch a video feed and then only ping the operator when something of relevance happens."

The Department of National Defence's IDEaS program, which asks Canadian companies for solutions to military challenges, has run a competition for that kind of video-feed monitor, seeking technology to "detect, recognize, and identify persons or objects of interest in a physical environment, and/or track identified persons and objects of interest using seamless information sharing across a decision network."

Toronto-based Ecopia AI passed through multiple stages to get to a $5.8-million "test drive" of its technology for extracting meaning from images (its intended commercial use is generally to make maps made from aerial pictures). Ecopia declined to talk about the potential military uses, with spokesperson Harneet Singh citing "the sensitivity involved around such engagements."

National Defence's own staff have observed that the IDEaS program, unlike similar ones run by our allies, doesn't have a final stage where the military buys the technology the program fosters. Purchases would have to go through Canada's regular military-procurement system. Which is not renowned. "The structures for procurement are built around bullets, tanks, hardware. They're not built around cyber, software, and rapid iteration cycles," says Daniel Araya, a senior fellow with the Centre for International Governance Innovation who studies AI governance, especially in international security.

Araya wrote a report for CIGI late in 2023 on AI in the Canadian military, based on workshops involving the defence establishment. One of its conclusions was that the military procurement system is no longer fit for purpose. "I don't want to pooh-pooh the military too much because I really think highly of the people in it, but in many, many respects, we have a fax-machine military for a cyber era," Araya says.

Buying new helicopters took Canada twenty-five years. We're now thirteen years into a process to buy new fighter jets, hoping to take delivery of the first one in 2026, and we bought more old fighter jets to supplement our decaying fleet of CF-18s. We've revised plans for new supply ships at least six times, starting in 2010, and we've extended the lease on a commercial freighter our navy has been using as a stopgap because we won't have the new ones for years more.

We set about upgrading infantry soldiers' communications equipment in 2005; although the department stopped updating the project website in 2021, the department said it hopes to have the gear fully in service by March 2024. Apple has released fifteen generations of iPhones in less time.

Blair acknowledged that the system needs reform and says the government has streamlined it to some degree already, cutting steps for low-complexity purchases and raising the threshold where a procurement requires oversight from outside the department to $7.5 million.

The paperwork isn't the only problem, Araya says: "It used to be that innovation was done inside the government in some form. Now, it's mostly done outside the government in the private sector. So the question is, how do we bridge those two spaces?"

And of course, Canada's defence budget is not large and is facing cuts, so the military cannot be a free-spending customer, even if it knew how.

Anduril, Eliot Pence's former company, has one answer: make what you think government buyers will want, rather than waiting for them to tell you (which was Steve Jobs's thinking, borrowed from Henry Ford). Sustaining a company until you have a compelling product takes a great deal of capital; Anduril has raised billions from sources like Peter Thiel's Founders Fund. "You need the warfighter, the entrepreneur, and the financier in the same room," says Pence, "and Canada has never, as far as I know, taken an institutional approach to convening those three."

The Canadian government has also signalled that for military contractors, selling products from Canada is a chancy business—something else that could discourage those who might develop cutting-edge defence technology here. An Ontario company, L3Harris Wescam, a subsidiary of US-based defence conglomerate L3Harris, sold optics that Turkey, a NATO ally, used in its popular Bayraktar drones. The federal government cancelled export permits based on "credible evidence" that Azerbaijan had used Bayraktars against Armenia in 2020.

That didn't happen with billions of dollars' worth of Canadian-made armoured vehicles bound for Saudi Arabia, but Prime Minister Justin Trudeau talked publicly about trying to find a way to stop those exports after the murder of Saudi journalist and dissident Jamal Khashoggi.

Araya pointed to one way the US manages to integrate innovation into its military. In-Q-Tel is a not-for-profit venture investment agency the US government launched in 1999 to find and back technologies useful for security and defence. Some call it the CIA's venture capital arm in Silicon Valley. It has taught the US military and security services how innovation happens, Araya says.

"They'll take in two or three developers that would otherwise work in their garage and say, 'We're going to deploy you inside the navy or inside the air force to help us build platforms.' That's just brilliant," he says.

The broader tech sector's qualms about working on deadly technology need to be addressed, as well, Araya believes. "We need to be able to justify our use of the military on ethical terms, right-values terms, and hopefully, build a relationship with a tech sector that is mutually beneficial," he says.

The US military's massive reach and budget put it on a different level from Canada's, which has to be choosier. In the 2022 federal budget, the Liberals promised to revise their 2017 national defence policy to deal with a global environment changed by the COVID-19 pandemic and Russia's full-scale invasion of Ukraine. The defence policy is a statement about what big tasks the Canadian Forces are supposed to be ready for and how the government intends to support those priorities. For instance, the government might make it a priority to protect the North, respond to natural disasters, or reinforce NATO's borders in Eastern Europe.

Although the 2017 document, entitled "Strong, Secure, Engaged," committed to buying all sorts of new equipment, including in fields where AI is now key, like cyber and signals intelligence, the phrase "artificial intelligence" does not appear anywhere in it. The government has not produced the promised revision yet, and last summer Trudeau shuffled out Anita Anand, the minister who had been overseeing it. Blair says the work is still underway.

That update will dictate where it makes sense to invest, says Araya. Canada's military can't be everything and as a NATO member with numerous allies, it doesn't need to be. But we could pursue brilliance in specific AI technology and aim to be the go-to supplier to allies. Surveillance, reconnaissance, and intelligence make sense as specialties, he says, given Canada's vast geography, sparse population, and increasing competition in the Arctic. "The Canadian military, in particular, is looking to expand in that space, to deploy drones in the Arctic, underwater," Araya says.

The important thing is to pick something and get moving. "Whether that's special forces or cyber or automation, or even logistics or whatever the hell it is, we should be really good at it—and probably the best at it," Araya says.

CHAPTER NINE

MORE COMPUTE, PLEASE

By Murad Hemmadi

Foteini Agrafioti interviewed a lot of machine-learning PhDs while assembling one of the larger corporate teams of AI researchers in the country. "The first question they ask you is, 'How many GPUs do you have?'" says Agrafioti, head of RBC's Borealis AI unit. It's an odd inquiry to make of a potential employer. But Agrafioti admits, "it's a scarce resource."

To train the models underpinning artificial intelligence systems and tools, developers need compute, the industry term for the processing power and infrastructure through which the programs run. Those stacks include software as well as graphics processing units (GPUs) and other chips.

Massive, multipurpose foundation models—like the large language models behind ChatGPT—need many times the compute that smaller ones require to train. Between September 2015 and February 2022, the amount they needed to get up to speed doubled about every ten months, according to a contemporary study. While training takes a lot of compute up front, "inferencing"—an application's output, like an answer to a query or a summary of a document—requires more processing power over time, as the system is used over and over.

Agrafiogi and other experts say that to thrive in the AI boom, Canada needs to ensure startups and researchers have access to the infrastructure to make those training runs, or to run applications that require a lot of cloud time. Other countries are spending significant sums to build new supercomputers and shore up their hardware supply chains. "Canada needs to figure out its computational power challenge," Agrafioti says.

Borealis has enough GPUs for its own work, which includes AI research and product development. In July 2020, RBC announced a deal with chipmaker Nvidia and the major software firm Red Hat for a private cloud setup. But Agrafioti, who also co-chairs the federal advisory council on AI, says she's concerned about whether smaller companies can access "this extremely expensive resource."

AI startups, particularly those in the buzzy generative space, have been raising huge sums of venture capital, even as the flow of money into other tech sub-sectors remains low. But many are spending a significant share of that funding on compute; partners at Silicon Valley financier Andreessen Horowitz recently estimated that for several firms, it's as high as four-fifths.

Some deals directly link the two. Microsoft has committed over US$11 billion to OpenAI, reportedly including credits for its Azure cloud. Anthropic selected Amazon Web Services (AWS) as its primary compute provider when the tech giant announced a US$4-billion investment in the firm.

Toronto generative AI startup Cohere has rejected deals with "money that needs to be recycled back into the investor," CEO Aidan Gomez wrote in a note to staff in November 2023. While such "arrangements of convenience" provide access to compute, companies can simply purchase it in the open market, and costs tend to drop over time, he says.

Intel's Canada country manager, Denis Gaudreault, has been getting a lot of calls about the semiconductor giant's AI chips and software recently, especially since ChatGPT debuted in November 2022: "People [are] realizing, 'I better get on that bandwagon, ASAP.'"

It's not just industry that needs compute infrastructure. Over the last two decades, researchers at Canadian universities made key breakthroughs in modern machine learning. But academia faces challenges to keep up with today's most popular systems, says Elissa Strome, executive director for the Pan-Canadian AI Strategy at CIFAR: "We don't have the computing facilities necessary to do generative AI on the same scale that OpenAI does." That's a problem, because independent researchers play a role in ensuring the technology is developed and deployed safely, she says.

Both new and established Canadian firms use the services of the very largest cloud providers, called hyperscalers, which include the US-based giants AWS, Azure, and Google Cloud. All three have programs offering credits for startups and researchers and have built multiple clusters of data centres in this country, allowing clients to meet any requirements to store information locally.

But Canada needs its own compute capacity for homegrown science and products, according to Dan Desjardins, CEO of Kingston's Distributive. "The Americans are making all the money—they're developing and deploying all the infrastructure," he says. Distributive's clients include hospitals and universities that use its software to split their AI and other workloads across the spare processing power of a network of computers, servers, and data centres.

Desjardins says the forty-person firm has raised about US$10 million to date. It is now part of a consortium trying to sell the federal government on a program to supplement Ottawa's existing science-compute system, operated by the Digital Research Alliance of Canada.

* * *

While several nations have launched AI strategies to earn a share of the technology's economic dividends, fewer have taken stock of the compute capacity available within their borders, according to a February 2023 paper published by the OECD. "This is akin to having a public health strategy without knowing how many hospital beds or ventilators you have," says Celine Caira, a Canadian economist at the organization who led work on the report.

The OECD has pushed policymakers to assess how much compute their countries have, how much they need, and what they can do to close any gap. The report also suggests countries consider factors like sustainability—data centres require a lot of power, which generates emissions. They also need security.

Some governments have pulled out their chequebooks. In November 2023, the UK announced it would spend £300 million ($506 million) on two supercomputers, which researchers can start using next summer to develop new AI applications and safety test foundational models. Countries are also offering billions to reshore production of semiconductors, critical components of compute hardware.

Beyond the big investments, some governments are trying to make better use of existing infrastructure, Caira says, citing moves like the EU opening its high-performance computing network for science to startups. "For researchers . . . you have quite a lot of capacity available," she says, noting that "many of these platforms were not necessarily available for commercial activities."

The federal government is working on the infrastructure issue, Innovation Minister François-Phillipe Champagne recently told The Logic, adding that he's discussed the subject with both startups and cloud providers. "If you want to be a leader in AI," he says, "you need to have affordable access to that computing capacity."

Desjardins says securing that processing power is crucial to AI-driven innovation, whether it's in medicine, aerospace, or beyond. "To compete, you must compute."

CHAPTER TEN

THE TAIWAN STRAIT

By David Reevely

Most of the supply chains that feed the growing artificial-intelligence industry run through Taiwan, whose territory is increasingly threatened by the Chinese government, which considers it a renegade province.

Voters in Taiwan are to choose a new president on January 13, 2024, in a ballot the main opposition party says will be a choice between war and peace. Even if that's overheated election rhetoric, any worsening of tensions could be devastating to nearly every industry that relies on microprocessors, including AI.

"Let's say something happens now and the entire supply chain from Taiwan is stopped," says Arun Iyengar, chief executive of Untether AI, a Toronto-based company that designs processors for neural networks, a form of artificial intelligence.

He paused.

"Wow, I mean," he chuckled uneasily, "that's just horrendous to imagine."

The possibilities for diversifying suppliers are negligible, at least over the next few years. For spinning up a domestic source, they're even worse. At best, Canada could play a role in building an alternative spread across multiple friendly countries to the one on a contested island about 180 kilometres from an increasingly adversarial regime.

Among other semiconductor makers, Taiwan is home to the Taiwan Semiconductor Manufacturing Company (TSMC), which is both a leading-edge manufacturer and a bulk supplier. Arguably the world's most advanced semiconductor manufacturer—only Samsung and Intel compete in the elite tier of the fabrication game—TSMC is also the dominant contract manufacturer of the parts that are critical to electronic systems of all kinds, including those that run artificial intelligence applications.

It operates a stunning fifteen fabricators, or "fabs," in Taiwan, plus two in mainland China and one in the United States.

A firm that relies on TSMC for its components, like Iyengar's, would need at least eighteen months to redesign them for another fabricator, "if you're really, really fast," he says. "It's a catastrophic situation if that ever came about."

The January 13 election pits the current vice-president, Lai Ching-te of the stridently anti-Beijing Democratic Progressive Party (DPP), against Ko Wen-je of the Taiwan People's Party and Hou Yu-ih of the Kuomintang, both of whom are seen as friendlier toward mainland China.

Despite his weak record on domestic economic issues, the DPP's Lai led narrowly in a poll conducted about six weeks in advance of the election, and after the opposition parties' effort to form an alliance blew up. Beijing was officially displeased at the result, painting the DPP as a destabilizing force that could push the region toward war.

Thinking of any of the potential next presidents as friends or enemies of Beijing is simplistic, warns Scott Simon, an anthropology professor at the University of Ottawa who shares the university's research chair in Taiwan studies (a post supported by the Taiwanese government). "None of them are saying, 'We want to be a province of the People's Republic of China.' None of them," he says. Nor is any candidate out to cross China's red line by declaring outright independence, he adds. The difference among the candidates is whether they think Taiwan's autonomy is best preserved with honey or with vinegar.

But Simon says even an administration warmer to Beijing could easily find itself in a tight spot. He points to a trade agreement between Taiwan, under a Kuomintang president, and the mainland that led to a 2014 occupation of Taiwan's parliament. It ended peacefully, but Simon thinks a repeat might not. "China has this anti-secession law that they passed, and it specifically says that if there's civil unrest in Taiwan, they can intervene," says Simon.

"The likelihood of a direct military conflict is still very, very small," says Jia Wang, deputy director of the University of Alberta's China Institute, who was born and educated in Beijing. "Compared to five or ten years ago, that probability is higher, though still very low."

Mainland China is Taiwan's biggest trading partner and people travel back and forth constantly, says Wang: "Taiwan and mainland China are two sides of the Taiwan Strait. There are just very many deep and broad ties between the two places."

Also militating in favour of peace: China depends on Taiwan's semiconductors, too. "Taiwan's chips power everything, including the US and Chinese militaries (China imports more chips than oil)," wrote Daniel Araya, a Canadian lawyer and technology consultant who works on AI issues and the US-China rivalry. But China is working mightily to free itself from dependence on Taiwan's foundries.

"Eventually—say by the end of the decade—China will have a completely independent chip ecosystem which will obviously mean a very different global order. At best, it could mean a completely bifurcated tech sector," says Araya. "As for Canada, we're just too inward-looking to appreciate how quickly things are changing."

The People's Republic would not have to invade, crossing a red line for the United States, to cause serious trouble. A naval blockade, even an undeclared partial one, could throttle exports from Taiwan or imports of vital raw materials and fuel. China imposed one after Nancy Pelosi, then the Speaker of the US House of Representatives, visited Taiwan in August 2022. "The Chinese military had multiple military drills around Taiwan Island. And that almost created a blockade, because nobody would want to get close to a military exercise," says Wang.

Canada is among the countries that have had sabre-rattling contests with China in nearby waters. As a result of the tensions, "most chip companies now are trying to figure out, OK, what are their options?" Iyengar says. There aren't a lot of good ones.

Hedging against the risk of trouble in Taiwan by "dual-sourcing" would mean redesigning products, because fabricators aren't interchangeable, says Hamid Arabzadeh, the CEO of Ottawa's Ranovus, which produces components for AI-oriented data centres and networks. Taiwanese chips, he says, are "not commodity chips. They are specialized."

The California-based processor companies AMD and Nvidia have helped to meet the high demand for compute spurred by AI's development. But "they are not commodity chips, either," Arabzadeh says, and the firms are in no position to replace Taiwan's production.

A company that has TSMC make high-end chips today would not find it easy to add a second supplier. Other makers could not simply take a design created for TSMC's production line and start churning out copies.

Redesigning for another manufacturer could take up to two years, and the buyer would lose the benefits of TSMC's advanced capabilities in the bargain, Arabzadeh said. The result would be less efficient, more expensive semiconductors, meaning a step back in technological time to a lower standard. "It's going to be a shock to the system," he says.

For most firms, a new source is out of the question, says Iyengar of Untether. "It costs anywhere from $50 million to $150 million, depending on the specific technology [level] you're targeting, to go build a chip. So even if you raise $150 million, you're barely able to do one properly, let alone two different designs for the same chip."

TSMC is building two fabs in Arizona, thanks in part to the US's CHIPS and Science Act, but the first is behind schedule and the next trick will be domestic "packaging," the final manufacturing stage. TSMC has put the price for the two fabs at US$40 billion.

"In the short term, there's not a ton Canada can do to beef up our own production," says Wang.

"It would be completely naive for Canada to go build a foundry in Canada," agrees Arabdzadeh. "We don't have the skill set." Nevertheless, Canada has specialty manufacturing facilities it could boost to promote its value in chip supply chains farther from China's reach, he says. For instance, the National Research Council has a foundry for chips that use lasers that could be the core of a competitively differentiated industry in compound semiconductors. "It's a different thing in the periodic table, but it is necessary—it coexists with semiconductors to enable AI workloads to be done," he says.

Advanced manufacturing for the packaging phase could also be a Canadian specialty. And the same CHIPS and Science Act that subsidizes large fabricators in the United States could support packaging in Canada. "Look at the strengths we have and double down on it, which would complement our allies, like the US, because they don't have the types of facilities that we have in Canada," says Arabdzadeh.

Hans Parmar, a spokesperson for Innovation Minister François-Philippe Champagne, made similar points in replying to questions about Canada's preparedness for a possible disruption in the supply of chips from Taiwan. "Canada is recognized as an R&D and design hub, with a reputation for world-leading expertise in high-value, specialized areas of semiconductor manufacturing such as compound semiconductor fabrication and advanced packaging," he wrote in an email.

Global Affairs Canada, meanwhile, touted Canada's international contribution to "critical minerals and semiconductor life-cycle value chains." Spokesperson Jean-Pierre Godbout wrote that Canada has just finished negotiations with Taiwan on a mutual investment deal and is "committed to growing economic and people-to-people ties with Taiwan while supporting its resilience."

That's likely Canada's best bet for now, says the University of Alberta's Wang. "We have some really cutting-edge AI research capacities and cutting-edge knowledge, but we're not a major player in the chipmaking industry, so we do rely on other countries to supply the most advanced chips, and chips overall," she says. "So, in many ways, to have a more peaceful world is in our interest."

CHAPTER ELEVEN

DOOM INC.

By Claire Brownell

In late May 2023, retired AI researcher Ramón Brena was checking his email at his home office in San Luis Potosí, Mexico, when a message popped up that got his attention. "Invitation to join Hinton, Bengio & Amodei," the subject line said. It came from Max Tegmark, president of the Future of Life Institute, a Narberth, Pennsylvania non-profit. Brena read on.

Two months earlier, Brena had joined one of those boldface names, Yoshua Bengio, in signing an open letter from the Future of Life Institute calling on AI labs to pause the training of more powerful AI systems out of concern for where they might lead. Now, the institute was leaning on the power of Bengio's involvement, along with that of fellow AI pioneer Geoffrey Hinton and Anthropic CEO Dario Amodei, to persuade him to sign something more.

"We think it is essential to also mainstream and legitimize debate about AI's most severe risks," the email said. Attached was a "new and concise" twenty-two-word statement on AI from the Center for AI Safety that read: "Mitigating the risk of extinction from AI should be a global priority alongside other societal-scale risks such as pandemics and nuclear war."

You may have heard of that twenty-two-word statement. It attracted international media attention. Ever since the launch of OpenAI's ChatGPT in November 2022, AI and the ominous warnings from big-name scientists that a technological apocalypse may be nigh have been staples of dinner table conversation.

The late 2023 drama at OpenAI, in which CEO Sam Altman was fired over reported tensions with safety-minded board members including

Canadian chief scientist Ilya Sutskever, only to be rehired four days later, highlighted the stakes at play and the deep concern some in the industry have for potential risks.

While Canada has played a key role in the development of AI, Hinton, Bengio, and Sutskever also stand among the most prominent global voices warning of the technology's potential dangers. They are part of a movement to convince lawmakers and the public that AI poses an existential threat to humanity. That movement is coordinated, well-funded, and animated by a shared set of ideas.

The Future of Life Institute and the Center for AI Safety have a common significant donor, the US granting organization Open Philanthropy. In 2017, Open Philanthropy donated US$30 million to OpenAI, then a startup with a declared mission of developing "safe and beneficial" artificial general intelligence. Open Philanthropy's former CEO, Holden Karnofsky, was once a board member at OpenAi.

Those concerned with AI's existential risks often call themselves longtermists or effective altruists. A more recent, and more pejorative descriptor is the term TESCREAL, an acronym coined by philosopher Émile Torres and former Google AI researcher Timnit Gebru to describe a bundle of philosophies: transhumanism, extropianism, singularitarianism, cosmism, rationalism, effective altruism, and longtermism.

One of the major beliefs the TESCREALists have in common, Torres says, is a heaven-or-hell view of technology: it will eventually transform humanity, either for better or worse. Get it right and we can collectively shed the prisons of our human bodies and, in the words of futurist Ray Kurzweil, "multiply our effective intelligence a billion-fold by merging with the intelligence we have created." Get it wrong and, if we're lucky, we could end up with superhuman AI treating us like pet Labradors. If we're unlucky, we could accidentally be wiped out if AI takes a well-meaning human instruction like "manufacture as many paperclips as possible" too literally.

"It's either going to be complete annihilation, or utopia," Torres says, summarizing the TESCREAList tension between longing for and fearing superintelligent AI. "Therefore, we should be careful in creating AGI so we get it right and get utopia—rather than end up just going extinct."

Hinton and Open Philanthropy did not respond to requests for comment. Bengio said in an emailed statement that he believes his work signing and promoting various open letters on AI risk "is essential to protect democracy, society, humanity and our shared future against AI's immediate and potential threats," but he is not affiliated with the Future of Life Institute or the Center for AI Safety and does not identify as an effective altruist.

While the Center for AI Safety did not provide an on-the-record response, Anthony Aguirre, executive director of the Future of Life Institute, said in an emailed statement that his organization has not received funding from Open Philanthropy since 2020 and is not affiliated with effective altruism. The institute reached out to some people in its network about signing the Center for AI Safety statement because it "reflected our shared goal of reducing the risks of the out-of-control, unchecked race to develop increasingly powerful advanced AI systems," he said.

Brena, the retired AI researcher, says he doesn't think it's productive to put too much focus on "the idea that AI is going to wipe humanity from Earth," an idea he considers "anthropomorphic" and not well founded in science. His other, more immediate concerns about artificial intelligence—like the potential for job loss and for tech companies to take people's data without consent—are the reason he signed the original open letter calling for a pause on the development of more powerful AI systems. He gave some thought to signing the second statement but was uneasy about it. He eventually decided against it. "I stayed with the feeling that something was off about this one," he says.

In addition to his concern that focusing on the extinction risk from AI distracted from the technology's present-day harms, he felt the comparison of AI risk to pandemics was manipulative, given the COVID-19 restrictions and waves of deaths the world had recently endured.

Brena was not aware that the Future of Life Institute and Center for AI Safety have both received funding from Open Philanthropy, which is in turn mainly funded by billionaire Facebook co-founder Dustin Moskovitz and his wife, Cari Tuna. The links between the organizations promoting an AI doom message deserve more scrutiny, he says.

"Following the money, where the support is actually coming from?" he says. "I think that's a very clever idea."

* * *

In the drizzle of a grey day in October 2023, AI Governance and Safety Canada executive director Wyatt Tessari L'Allié stepped onto a platform on Parliament Hill to speak at the AI Safety and Ethics Rally. He had to make himself heard over the din of another, larger, unaffiliated demonstration happening at the same time. "Hello, everyone," he joked into a microphone. "I made the very wise decision of bringing paper notes on a rainy day."

Only about twenty people in total attended the rally, one of a handful held at cities around the world that day to call for a ban on the creation of superintelligent AI. L'Allié says his Ottawa-based organization isn't itself calling for a pause on AI development, but he shares the concerns of those who are.

L'Allié used to think climate change was the defining issue of our time, leading him to run for the federal Green Party and speak at environmental rallies. In 2015, he started reading books that convinced him that AI risk, not climate change, is his generation's defining issue.

One of the books he read was *Global Catastrophic Risks*, co-edited by the University of Oxford philosopher Nick Bostrom. The book includes an essay by Eliezer Yudkowsky, a co-founder of Berkeley's Machine Intelligence Research Institute, which argues that assuming superintelligent AI will be friendly to humans "implies an obvious path to global catastrophe." Yudkowsky makes the case that it's imperative to figure out how to make sure AI is aligned with human values before we develop it.

Bostrom and Yudkowsky are foundational and controversial thinkers in the movement to influence public opinion and policy on AI existential risk. Both have strong links to the so-called TESCREAL bundle of philosophies.

In January 2023, Bostrom's views attracted scrutiny after Torres publicized a racist email he had sent to a listserv in the 1990s; he used a racial slur and said he believes Black people are less intelligent than white people. Bostrom apologized in a response, calling the email "disgusting" and stating that his use of a racial slur was "repulsive" and that the email does not accurately represent his past or current views. He did not explicitly disavow the idea that some racial groups are less intelligent than others.

Both Yudkowsky and Bostrom are transhumanists, a philosophy that advocates for the use of technology to transcend the limits of our bodies. Transhumanists often hold a quasi-religious belief in a coming end time brought on by the singularity, or the merging of human intelligence and artificial superintelligence.

Yudkowsky is perhaps better known as creator of the blog LessWrong, "a community dedicated to improving our reasoning and decision-making." LessWrong is affiliated with the rationalist movement—which attempts to remove bias from thinking and see the world as it actually is—and also the effective altruism community, which encourages people to orient their careers and charitable giving towards doing the maximum amount of good in the world.

Prominent effective altruist William MacAskill popularized the concept of longtermism in his 2022 book *What We Owe the Future*, which argues we should focus on actions with the greatest positive impact on distant generations—including preventing human extinction at the hands of AI. Under his influence, effective altruists have mostly shifted their focus from improving health in impoverished nations to AI safety.

These philosophies have drawn considerable criticism. The trans-humanist project of enhancing human intelligence and eliminating disabilities has been called eugenicist, a charge that has also been levelled at Bostrom for fretting about less intelligent people outbreeding the smart. Many have held up the downfall of effective altruist Sam Bankman-Fried, who claimed to have launched the failed crypto-trading platform FTX in order to make as much money as possible and give it away, as an example of how the philosophy, taken to extremes, can end up looking a lot like "the ends justify the means."

Criticism of effective altruism spiked again in the wake of the OpenAI boardroom drama. In an opinion piece for *The Information*, OpenAI investor Vinod Khosla said the firm's "board members' religion of 'effective altruism' and its misapplication could have set back the world's path to the tremendous benefits of artificial intelligence." Aidan Gomez of Cohere, Shopify CEO Tobi Lütke, Coinbase CEO Brian Armstrong, and prominent tech reporter Kara Swisher also criticized the philosophy as the crisis played out.

Critics have also noted that focusing on people in the far-off future has the convenient side effect of giving those in positions of wealth and privilege an excuse to avoid doing something about the problems faced by those less fortunate today. After *The New York Times* published an article in May 2023 in which Hinton said he had left his job at Google to speak freely about the dangers of AI, some of his former colleagues expressed outrage that he hadn't spoken up when Google AI ethics researchers lost their jobs after publishing a paper about the harms the technology poses to marginalized communities, or when employees organized a walkout over the company's contracts with the US Department of Defense.

Despite its critics, this stew of ideas is everywhere in the world of Big Tech. Prominent investor Peter Thiel and Russian-Canadian Ethereum co-founder Vitalik Buterin have expressed thoughts consistent with aspects of rationalism, transhumanism, or longtermism.

Two other noted Canadians, Elon Musk and his former partner Claire Boucher, known professionally as the musician Grimes, reportedly met after tweeting the same pub referencing a LessWrong post about AI risk. Musk and Buterin have made significant donations to the Future of Life Institute, the organization behind the open letter calling for a six-month pause on AI development.

The boardroom coup at OpenAI that captivated the tech world's attention appears to have been rooted in these philosophies, as well. Tasha McCauley and Helen Toner, two of the board members involved in firing Altman who were later replaced, have links to organizations that are backed by or explicitly affiliated with effective altruism, while Sutskever has expressed views about AI risk that are consistent with those held by effective altruists and longtermists. Sutskever had spearheaded a technical breakthrough (a model called Q*, or "Q-Star") prior to the boardroom coup, *The Information* reported, raising concerns among safety-focused staff about whether the company had sufficient safeguards in place.

Even Altman, who appears to have been on the other side of the effective altruist-linked campaign to reduce AI risk during the debacle, has expressed views consistent with other letters in the TESCREAL bundle. Altman was an effusive fan of the now-defunct rationalist blog Slate Star Codex, and is one of twenty-five people who paid US$10,000 to join a waitlist for a transhumanist startup that proposes to euthanize customers and preserve their brains in the hopes of one day uploading their consciousnesses into the cloud.

This year, these philosophies have begun to receive mainstream attention from lawmakers and the public in the form of concern about AI's apocalyptic potential.

Most of the organizations behind the UK's high-profile AI Safety Summit held in November 2023 have links to effective altruism. Open Philanthropy, the effective altruist grant-maker funding the organizations behind the AI risk letters, is also bankrolling the salaries of tech fellows working in the US Senate and other government departments. In Canada, Open Philanthropy has funded at least six grants to researchers at Canadian universities and institutions working on projects related to AI ethics and alignment with human values.

At the AI Safety Summit, Canada's Innovation Minister François-Philippe Champagne says he's considering joining the UK and the US in creating AI safety organizations. In an interview with The Logic, Champagne said "everyone acknowledged" AI's potential existential risk to humanity at the summit, "and we are determined to take action."

Kyunghyun Cho, an AI researcher and an associate professor at New York University, says he believes the abundant funding from effective altruist organizations is influencing junior researchers' decisions about whether to enter the field and what type of research to pursue. "Academics are always craving funding," he says. "The more junior faculty members moving into this field of AI, they probably have been influenced somewhat by the abundance of funding."

L'Allié has himself been the beneficiary of the effective altruism movement's deep pockets. In 2022, he received two grants of US$87,000 and US$17,000 from the Long-Term Future Fund, an EA-linked endowment that "aims to positively influence the long-term trajectory of civilization" and receives funding from Open Philanthropy. The money helped get the organization off the ground, although L'Allié noted the grants were for individuals and not AIGS Canada, which he says is funded by small- and medium-sized donors and does not accept foreign funding.

Asked if he's heard of the acronym TESCREAL and what he thinks about criticisms of effective altruism and related philosophies, L'Allié laughed. "I think it's entirely valid to question the motives of people," he says. "Big Tech has a lot of problems, and we should be very on our guard." But he doesn't see much to worry about: "The people that I've met in the EA movement, for the most part, they're well-meaning nerds."

L'Allié says he's excited about the momentum that's developed behind the concept of AI safety this year, a formerly niche and technical issue. The open letters, signed by scientific luminaries such as Bengio and Hinton, played a huge role in changing the conversation, he says. "It's huge. It's just logically gratifying to know that we weren't crazy."

* * *

While Hinton and Bengio, two of the three Canadian godfathers of IA, are ringing alarms about AI's potential risks to humanity, the third, Richard Sutton, has serious concerns about the growing safety movement. Sutton says Bengio approached him about signing the Future of Life statement calling for a six-month pause on AI development. His answer was a resounding no. "I wasn't interested at all," he says. "I guess I was not approached on the second one because it was clear what my position was going to be."

Sutton believes the statements are part of a coordinated public opinion campaign: "A concerted effort in a very deliberate way to change the Overton window. And I'm very unhappy with it."

Sutton has put considerable effort into understanding the increasingly influential conversation around AI risk, reading books by Bostrom, Yudkowsky, and Future of Life Institute president Max Tegmark (who in June shared a stage with Bengio at a June Munk Debate event where they argued in favour of the resolution "AI research and development poses an existential threat"). He has come away unimpressed.

Sutton says he found implausible the authors' hypothetical scenarios where runaway AI could lead to disaster. "I look for it, and I do not see an argument," he says. "Instead, there just seems to be people manipulating. They're using all the levers to generate fear."

It's unclear whether Hinton and Bengio share the worldview of Bostrom, Yudkowsky, Tegmark, and others, or just their concern about AI risks. In a blog post, Bengio described a book by computer scientist Stuart Russell—whose Center for Human-Compatible AI is funded by Open Philanthropy and Effective Altruism Funds, the same bundle of grantmaking reserves linked to the movement that funded Ottawa's L'Allié—as being a turning point in his "awareness of a possible existential risk for humanity if we do not maintain control over superhuman AI systems." Bengio's statement to The Logic did not directly address a question asking what impact, if any, TESCREAList thinking has had on his views.

Sutton says he's dismayed by Bengio and Hinton's willingness to lend credence to the global campaign on AI risk. "Yoshua and Geoff have gone to the side of fear, and I'm just extremely disappointed in both of them," he says. "They also do not provide any worthwhile arguments, in my opinion."

Other figures in Canada's AI community are similarly concerned about the credibility and mainstream attention the movement is receiving, due in part to Bengio and Hinton. Amir Hajian, vice-president of data science at Toronto-based Arteria AI, says the success of the AI doom message may help companies with a lead—such as OpenAI, whose executives signed the Center for AI Safety statement—keep their dominant position.

"It looks like a way for Big Tech to build a moat around itself," he says. Stringent regulations about safety and alignment are expensive to follow, he says. "You're eliminating everyone else who doesn't have big money, like us."

Nicole Janssen, co-CEO of Edmonton-based applied AI company AltaML, says Canadian policymakers don't seem to be fixating on the doomsday message, to her relief. "Canada's government recognizes that this is the biggest opportunity we will have as a country in our lifetime," she says. "If we do not grab a hold of this opportunity, we will not compete."

However, Bengio and Hinton do have the ears of lawmakers in Canada and abroad. At the UK AI Safety Summit, Champagne cited Bengio's recent appointment to chair an international study of the potential risks and promise of frontier AI systems as an example of how Canada is "front and centre when it comes to thought leadership" on the issue.

Bengio and Hinton are continuing to lend the power of their names to open letters on AI risks. Both scientists signed another in late October 2023 and Bengio signed one more in advance of the UK AI Safety Summit. The first of these, "Managing AI Risks in an Era of Rapid Progress," laid out the heaven-and-hell case once again. Get AI right and we could end sickness, save the environment, and improve our quality of life; get it wrong and we could end up unleashing a malevolent superintelligence that could take control of our financial systems, militaries, and supply chains.

The all-powerful AI described in these letters may be around the corner, or it may never arrive. But the movement working to convince us to fear it is very much here. The world will have to rely on human—not artificial—intelligence to decide whether to dismiss it or start building bunkers.

David Kawai contributed to the reporting for this chapter

CHAPTER TWELVE

BRAVE STEPS, NEW WORLD

By Murad Hemmadi

British Prime Minister Rishi Sunak was at the centre—this was, after all, his summit. Two chairs over, on either side, were European Commission President Ursula von der Leyen and US Vice-President Kamala Harris. Their presence alone made the meeting at Bletchley Park in Milton Keynes important.

Few inhabitants of the London commuter town would recognize the Canadian computer scientist seated at Sunak's left. But without the work and words of Yoshua Bengio, the world leaders and technology executives at Bletchley Park might not have assembled to talk artificial intelligence on that drizzly Thursday.

Over dozens of years and papers, a community of researchers around the Montreal professor and his Toronto contemporary, Geoffrey Hinton, helped shift AI from science fiction to commercial fact. Companies are now hustling to develop and sell a bewildering range of applications and governments see the potential to grow their economies and solve significant societal challenges. Yet countries seeking AI's promise are also being confronted by the technology's potential perils. Bengio and Hinton are leading there, too, lending their voices to caution against unbridled development of AI. Policymakers around the world are paying heed.

Sunak's meeting, the November 2023 UK AI Safety Summit, held over two days at Bletchley Park, was the first ever global summit on artificial intelligence. It brought together global leaders and tech superstars such as Elon Musk and Sam Altman to attempt to reach agreement on issues that many nations have been working on independently.

"You're seeing a lot of governments trying to throw their hat in the ring," says Amba Kak, executive director of the AI Now Institute, a policy think tank in New York. The result has been a cacophony of proposals and initiatives.

The European Union is in the late stages of adopting its AI Act, which would impose high fines for violations and outright ban applications like live facial recognition. Officials from the continent have been working to popularize its approach in other capitals. In Washington, the Biden administration began with voluntary guardrails, and is now looking at firmer rules, as is Congress.

The US also hosts most of the field's largest firms, who are pushing their own regulatory models. These concerns some observers. The AI Now Institute's Kak says policymakers must avoid letting industry set the terms of AI governance, and should prioritize binding, national regulation. "We are at risk if all of these governments come together [to] agree on some high-level international principles, [then] go home and think they've done their job."

Sunak and his government have positioned themselves as a broker between various countries' approaches to AI governance. At the summit, digital ministers shared roundtables with tech CEOs, researchers, and some civil-society representatives to discuss risks, particularly those raised by so-called frontier AI, the multi-purpose models on which tools like ChatGPT run.

The summit got a lot of governments thinking together about AI policy, says Rebecca Finlay, who chaired one of the roundtables. She is the Canadian CEO of Partnership on AI, a San Francisco non-profit that develops standards to guide its members, including firms, academic institutes and civil-society groups. "It's not like we're starting from scratch," Finlay says, but the meetings did create more room for cross-border conversation.

The US competed for attention: many attendees broke away from the summit on the first day to watch a speech by Harris in London, where the vice-president made the case that bias, errors, and deepfakes are as pressing and existential as the prospect of machine-made cyberattacks or bioweapons.

Those competing priorities were also central to the discussion back at Bletchley Park, says Cohere CEO Aidan Gomez. Plenty of participants were pushing back on "doomsday scenarios" to focus on more imminent risks.

In the end, British brokerage yielded deals. Twenty-nine governments represented at the summit signed a pledge of greater cooperation on AI safety. Sunak's team counted it as a bit of a coup that the US and China appeared together on both the document and the stage. Eight leading AI firms agreed to let the new UK and US AI safety institutes test their models before release. "Considering where this whole debate was before the prime minister intervened in the summer, I think it's been a real triumph," Matt Clifford, Sunak's summit representative, told reporters.

If Britain made a star turn on the Bletchley Park stage, Canada, too, was a notable presence. Innovation Minister François-Philippe Champagne and his team were active in the summit's group chats, side meetings, and mainstage appearances. "When Canada speaks on AI," says Champagne, "people definitely listen."

The minister wants Canada to have a lead role in assuring AI's responsible use and regulation. "We're very much front and centre," he says, citing his government's role in establishing the Global Partnership on Artificial Intelligence, another twenty-nine-government group fostering international cooperation. "All these initiatives are complementary."

Indeed, international AI undertakings and panels are proliferating almost as fast as the technology. The OECD has a set of AI principles. So do the G20 and the G7. And the United Nations recently appointed its own group to "bridge other existing and emerging initiatives." Canada is involved in all of it. "We're not watching on television—we're actually in the room," Simon Kennedy, deputy minister of Innovation, Science and Economic Development Canada, told an audience of business executives in November 2023.

As proof of this influence, a source familiar with Ottawa's approach pointed to the overlap between Canada's code of conduct on advanced AI systems, launched in September 2023, and the G7 version, published the following month. Both include commitments for organizations building such tools as well as those using them. (The US domestic equivalent focuses on developers.) Canada pushed for the distinction in the G7 document, said the source, who requested anonymity to discuss the process.

Notwithstanding the government's efforts, the Canadian who will play the lead role in the next major stage of international AI governance is the private citizen who sat next at Sunak on the stage at Bletchley Park. The British prime minister announced that the Université de Montréal's Bengio will hold the pen on a "state-of-the-science" report examining the capabilities of frontier systems. The document, designed to inform policymaking, is to be presented at a follow-on summit in 2024.

Champagne pointed to the appointment as evidence that Canada is showing "thought leadership and excellence" in AI. Gomez describes Bengio as "among the best scientists in our space and very well qualified to lead the initiative," adding, "He's certainly inclined towards doomsday scenarios—which I hold out hope will change."

Bengio himself says this country can play a part in AI safety, just as it did in the technology's development. "We're lucky in Canada to have an amazing talent pool that could contribute to [solving] this global problem and keep Canada in the lead in AI."

Whether Canada's leadership with be exerted most on the side of development or caution remains to be seen. Some in the sector already believe Ottawa is over-reaching on the side of safety. "Let other countries regulate while we take the more courageous path and say 'come build here,'" Shopify CEO Tobi Lütke tweeted when the code was announced, declining to sign.

Toronto's ADA committed to the guardrails, but CEO Mike Murchison thinks the country needs a tone shift. "We could be much more opportunity-focused, and much less risk averse," he says, citing potential gains in productivity and quality of life.

In September, the Council of Canadian Innovators, a scale-up lobby group, called for Ottawa to move faster on regulating AI and give firms more freedom to launch less-risky applications. Prolonged uncertainty could cost Canada, the group warned—the United States is just a quick re-incorporation away. To slow the flow, it's also lobbying officials for an AI commercialization and IP strategy.

Champagne, meanwhile, is keeping his options open. He speaks about the "need to move from uncertainty and fear to opportunities," yet insists on a balanced approach. "Without trust, it's going to be very difficult to perceive the opportunities, whether it's in the field of research, education, or climate change."

The stakes, and the stage, could hardly be bigger. AI will grow our economies and save us from our worst social and environmental predicaments. Or AI will fracture our workforces, splinter our societies, and create unforeseen catastrophes. Wherever along the spectrum the future falls, you're likely to find Canadians in the spotlight.

The country has retained its central place in the AI research community, says Gomez. That's what started all of this. The next, critical phase of the transformative technology will be to realize the rewards while handling the risks. "Canada," Gomez says, "has an important leadership role to play on the global stage."

AFTERWORD

By Kevin Carmichael

In the days leading up to the November 2023 AI Safety Summit in the UK, there was a clear tension between those who believe artificial intelligence will be an unprecedented boon to society and those who fear it will end the world. Canadian AI pioneer Yoshua Bengio, one of the most vocal of the doomsayers, will now help guide the thinking of the world's governments on how to regulate the technology. I don't have Bengio's command of the subject, but I'm drawn more to the arguments of his peers who believe in AI's vast economic upside.

Maybe I should be among those who see AI as a threat. As a journalist, some of my competitive advantage over technology eroded when OpenAI took down the fence that had confined ChatGPT to munching on data produced before September 2021. Want real-time news? Ask Bing, which now runs on ChatGPT-4.

Adding value to the first draft of history is getting harder. I've typed enough words about the Bank of Canada and the Federal Reserve to play a credible "central-bank watcher" on social media. But JPMorgan Chase is already using a ChatGPT-based AI to analyze Fed statements and speeches for clues on where interest rates are headed. And researchers at the Bank of Canada showed in 2022 that it's possible to use face-recognition and voice-recognition technology to anticipate how US Federal Reserve chair Jerome Powell's *emotions* during congressional testimony will affect stock prices.

Whatever existential angst I'm feeling is an example of the fear and loathing that comes with every big technological or structural change, as Matt Ridley showed in *How Innovation Works*.

Early in the nineteenth century, the Luddites wrecked the looms, then lost momentum when the broader public realized the looms meant more cotton—of an acceptable or better quality—for less money. A more productive and profitable textile industry generated previously unimaginable scale and profits, leaving the economy wealthier. That wealth generated more jobs than existed before and the Luddites were eventually forgotten, until scribes needed a metaphor for technophobia at the beginning of the next period of disruption.

Economist Tyler Cowen argues that AI will make society vastly more intelligent. Most everyone will have access to a personal research assistant, speechwriter, and life planner. That's bad news for anyone who had hoped for a career doing the bidding of researchers, speech givers, or the habitually disorganized. But it's undeniably good for everyone else.

A few years ago, I noticed a spot on my back. It grew, and my partner nudged me to ask my family doctor about it. My doctor was pretty sure it was nothing, but he put me in line to see a dermatologist. In Quebec, where I live, wait times for a specialist are between three days and twelve months, according to the provincial government. My appointment, when it arrived several months later, lasted less than five minutes. I had barely removed my shirt when the dermatologist said the spot was nothing but a sign of age. I apologized for taking up valuable space in his calendar. He told me I shouldn't worry; he and his colleagues see a dozen cases like mine a day.

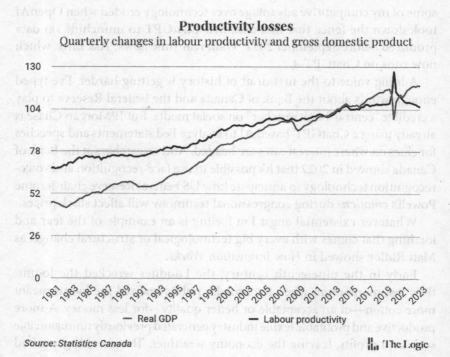

Productivity losses
Quarterly changes in labour productivity and gross domestic product

Source: Statistics Canada

Think about that for a minute. Highly trained professionals who wake up every day facing backlogs they will never clear are spending significant time on age spots. If machine learning can see into the souls of central bankers, then it surely could be used by a nurse practitioner or some other technician to help members of an aging society avoid further clogging the health-care system's waiting lists.

AI won't turn us all into doctors. But it could let someone with a base level of knowledge do things that currently require over a decade of post-secondary training. Across society, talent would be able to maximize its potential. Everyone would be rewarded with more time, money, or both. Society would be healthier and wealthier, and the economy would be stronger.

Unfortunately, Canada isn't good at taking advantage of technological change. It's one of the reasons—and maybe the biggest one—why the amount of economic output per hour worked had been declining for more than a year by the summer of 2023, according to Statistics Canada's quarterly measure of labour productivity. The decline can only be interpreted as a marker of fundamental weakness.

"This country has actually done a very good job of growing by adding workers," Bank of Canada governor Tiff Macklem told the House finance committee in October 2023. "Companies are good at hiring workers and integrating them into the workforce, and that has really been the key to our growth. What has been disappointing is we've been much less successful in growing output per worker, or productivity. Why that really matters is that higher productivity pays for higher wages; it's the source of sustained increases in our standard of living."

We're testing the limits of the growth-by-hiring model. The economy slowed to a crawl as 2023 wound down, yet the job vacancy rate was still considerably higher than it was before the pandemic. That suggests demographics are making it harder for companies to satisfy demand by hiring more people. Immigration Minister Marc Miller's recent decision to cap immigration at current levels suggests that employers won't be able to fill gaps with temporary foreign workers or by raiding other countries for talent.

Productivity is about more than technology, of course. We reduce the supply of skilled workers by letting professional associations control accreditation, which has the effect of constraining supply by blocking talent from maximizing its potential. Regulation by multiple levels of

Help still wanted
Monthly Canadian job vacancies, all industries

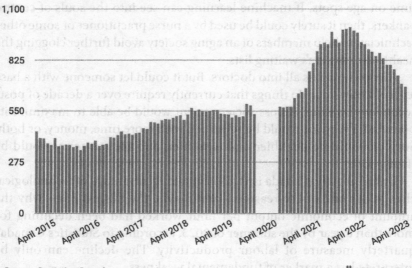

Source: Statistics Canada

government frustrates innovation, and our relatively small market dulls the incentive to invest at home when opportunities across the border in the US are so much greater.

A technology as powerful as AI could help companies power through such friction, turning disincentives into mere excuses. AI will make hundreds of thousands of us redundant in our current positions. But there's every reason to believe that it will create just as many opportunities—*if* employers embrace it.

In Canada, the biggest risk AI poses is that companies will balk at doing so.

Kevin Carmichael is The Logic's economics columnist and editor-at-large.

APPENDIX

CANADIANS TO WATCH

By *Murad Hemmadi & Claire Brownell*

The country's three AI pioneers—Geoffrey Hinton, Yoshua Bengio, and Richard Sutton—remain hugely influential in the sector and much covered. But plenty of other researchers across the country are advancing the field through their research, entrepreneurialism, and policy work.

Here are some of the key players shaping Canadian AI.

The founders

Aidan Gomez, Nick Frosst and Ivan Zhang (Cohere)

Canada has its very own generative AI standard bearer in Cohere. Clients use the Toronto scale-up's technology to add machine-made text to such products and services as predictive copywriting and search that considers meaning rather than just keywords.

"The technology that we're building on is the same technology that we see emerging now, both in Big Tech as well as in some other startups like ourselves—these big language models trained on the web," says CEO Aidan Gomez. "What Cohere does is really try to present them to the world in a way that is maximally accessible."

At Google Brain, Gomez was on the team that published what's come to be known as the "transformer paper" in 2017. The device it proposed forms the basis for the large language models (among others) that underpin most current generative systems. Gomez and Ivan Zhang started Cohere in September 2019, with third co-founder Nick Frosst joining them shortly thereafter.

Backed by Toronto's Radical Ventures, the firm has raised capital from the likes of Index Ventures, Salesforce Ventures, and Tiger Global. In June 2023, the firm announced a US$270-million Series C led by Montreal-based Inovia Capital.

Cohere's plans don't end at language. "The most exciting project in AI is modelling the internet," says Gomez.

Shelby Austin (Arteria AI)

Years before the current hype hit, Shelby Austin was alive to AI's potential to help automate and streamline the busywork of large enterprises.

Most of the data that corporations hold is unstructured, contained in communications or files that aren't indexed or linked together. Arteria AI's platform takes in information from financial-services firms' systems, staff, and clients, then produces analytics, paperwork, and recommendations. A bank might use the technology to handle the documentation to onboard one customer faster, or monitor transactions with another, explained CEO Austin.

Clients include Goldman Sachs and Citi. "Everyone cares who the large banks use to help with their technological challenges," Austin says. While Arteria's technology could be adopted well beyond financial services, she noted that the market for AI and automation in its current target sector is projected to be worth hundreds of billions over the next decade.

Austin, a lawyer, spun Arteria out of Deloitte in October 2020. She'd led the AI practice at the consulting giant, which she'd joined in 2014 when it acquired her previous startup. Detaching Arteria from Deloitte allowed it to scale up and raise outside capital, she says. In October 2023, the firm closed a US$30-million Series B from Citi, GGV Capital, and BDC Capital, among others.

While the company uses LLMs, model makers like OpenAI aren't a threat to Arteria, according to Austin. "Domain-specific AI is outperforming generalist AI," she says, noting that new applications will struggle to replicate her firm's grasp of the workflow requirements and business processes of corporate investment banking.

Arteria is staffing up its sales teams in financial hubs London and New York and taking a patient approach to growth. "We're trying to build a company that will be here in ten or twenty years, which is a different way of building than one that you plan to exit quickly," she says.

Charles Onu (Ubenwa)

Charles Onu wants to do for babies' cries what smartwatches have done for adults' heart rates and oxygen saturation levels. Ubenwa, his Montreal-based startup, applies AI to analyze the infant noises for health insights.

In the early months of a child's life, wailing isn't just a cry for attention, says Onu. It's an involuntary action triggered by the central nervous system. "The baby has no control over it," he says. "They can't choose when to cry, how much to cry, how loud to cry." Medical conditions modify those sounds, something an experienced doctor or midwife might identify. But a parent's untrained ear might not be able to hear what's wrong. So in May 2023, eleven-person Ubenwa launched an app for caregivers that uses its AI models to interpret the sounds.

The data to train the system—recordings and clinical annotations—came from pediatricians at five hospitals across Brazil, Canada, and Nigeria. The firm and its research collaborators initially focused on brain-injury detection, and recently published a paper on the outcomes of ventilator tube removals in the journal *Pediatric Research*.

"My research has always been at the intersection of machine learning and medicine," Onu says. He did his PhD in machine learning at McGill University under Doina Precup, who also heads Google DeepMind's Montreal office; she's now an adviser to his firm. Onu launched this iteration of Ubenwa out of Mila, the research institute McGill shares with Université de Montréal.

In July 2022, the startup raised US$2.5 million in a pre-seed round from Radical Ventures, Mila's Bengio, and other AI researchers. "We've crossed the venture Rubicon—there's no going back," he says, noting a seed round will follow soon. Ubenwa will also eventually enter regulatory processes and clinical trials with the US Federal Drug Administration and Health Canada so that it can offer its technology in medical devices.

Arun Iyengar and Martin Snelgrove (Untether); Jim Keller (Tenstorrent)

The advent of AI has realigned the semiconductor sector, altering decades-old hierarchies among the industry's titans and seeding a new crop of chip startups designing components specifically for machine-learning workloads. Two nascent firms a dozen kilometres apart in Toronto are among the most promising.

Semiconductor superconnector Martin Snelgrove co-founded Untether in June 2017 to create "a new generation of computer architecture that's built around the mathematics that neural nets like to do." The technology's users include General Motors's Canadian Technical Centre and other carmakers, which are testing the chips in autonomous-vehicle perception systems, as well as defence contractors and financial-services firms.

Snelgrove is now CTO, after Arun Iyengar, a veteran business executive, joined Untether as CEO in September 2019. The firm's forthcoming second-generation chipset will be "the most efficient" of its peers, Iyengar says.

Tenstorrent is the other Toronto AI semiconductor star. AMD alumnus Ljubisa Bajic founded the firm in March 2016, but has since stepped back from an operational role. Palo Alto-based Jim Keller took over as CEO in January 2023. The former Apple, Intel, and Tesla executive was an early investor in Tenstorrent. The startup's Grayskull cards are designed for servers running machine-learning systems. LG Electronics has licensed Tenstorrent's technology to develop chiplets for its TV and auto products.

Developing semiconductors is a capital-intensive business, and both firms have closed mega-rounds in the last two years, with Tenstorrent taking in more than US$300 million from the likes of Fidelity Investments, Hyundai, and Samsung, and Untether raising US$125 million, co-led by Intel Capital.

The funder

Jordan Jacobs (Radical Ventures)

AI remains a rare bright spot in a gloomy global venture capital market. Radical Ventures, founded in 2017, got in early on many of the startups in the field that are still raising mega-rounds today. Jordan Jacobs is co-founder and managing partner of the Toronto financier. "All the software in the world gets replaced by AI in the next decade," he predicts. Radical plans to own a piece of many of the companies running or selling the technology for that transformation. The firm's public portfolio includes nearly four dozen firms, mostly in Canada and the US. Notable names north of the border include tissue-printing firm Aspect Biosciences, Untether, autonomous-vehicle startup Waabi, and quantum computing company Xanadu.

And then there's Cohere. In mid-2017, Jacobs was running the startup Layer 6 when he read a preprint version of the "transformer paper" co-authored by Gomez. He perceived in it "the next iteration of AI." It helped seal his decision to sell Layer 6—TD Bank acquired it in January 2018—and convert Radical into a full-time institutional fund. The firm's investment in Cohere is a bet that LLMs will be transformative, but that there's a big space in the market for a provider not tied to Microsoft, as is OpenAI.

Jacobs is himself prominent in Toronto's AI ecosystem as one of the key figures behind the creation of the Vector Institute. Radical may be headquartered in the city, but Jacobs wants to be "a global elite fund" winning the best AI deals. The firm has added a raft of high-profile partners, including ex-McKinsey chief Dominic Barton, pioneering researcher Fei Fei Li, and former DeepMind executive Aaron Rosenberg. Radical recently closed a third US$550-million venture fund.

Investors have jumped on the perceived market opportunity of AI, and some will lose money, Jacobs acknowledged. "We have the technical depth to understand what's real," he says, noting that Radical's partners have experience with "how to write the software to wrap around the algorithms [and] sell it into enterprise."

The policy shapers

Samir Chhabra, Surdas Mohit, and Jaxson Khan (Government of Canada)

Innovation Minister François-Philippe Champagne introduced Bill C-27, which includes the Artificial Intelligence and Data Act (AIDA), in June 2022. The proposed law has been a flashpoint in the field, with business executives expressing concern that it is too vague, and rights advocates warning it does not adequately protect vulnerable populations. Prominent academics like Bengio, meanwhile, have urged Parliament to pass it as quickly as possible.

Federal officials Chhabra, Mohit, and Khan didn't write AIDA, but they're at the forefront of the government's efforts to explain it to industry and civil society, and revise it to address some of the feedback.

Samir Chhabra is director general of the Marketplace Frameworks Policy Branch at Innovation, Science and Economic Development Canada (ISED), charged with the upkeep of the laws and regulations in

Champagne's portfolio. He took the job in November 2022, after stints at the federal employment and finance departments.

Surdas Mohit has been acting director for AI and data policy in the branch's privacy directorate since June 2022.

Jaxson Khan joined Champagne's office as a policy advisor in March 2022 from Toronto tech startup Fable, having previously worked at Influitive and Nudge AI.

As written, AIDA would leave details of which systems it will cover to future regulations, which ISED would have two years to draft. With industry pushing for specificity, however, the Liberal government has signalled that it will try to amend the law to set out classes of covered tools, including ones used in employment and health-care decisions, as well as social media algorithms.

"We are alive to the concerns that have been raised about the bill," says a senior government official, whom the department made available on condition they not be named. Still, "there is increasingly broad agreement across civil society and business leaders that regulating AI should be a current priority."

Teresa Scassa (University of Ottawa); Christelle Tessono et al.

Teressa Scassa, a University of Ottawa law professor, dubbed AIDA "statutory Mad Libs" shortly after it was tabled. While "AI is big and the risks it poses are big," the legislation doesn't adequately address those downsides, the oft-cited privacy expert says.

Passing "an empty shell of a law" and then filling it in via regulations doesn't make the rulemaking process more agile, argues Scassa. Nor will it resolve what she considers problematic provisions written into the bill, such as giving enforcement responsibility to the same minister charged with promoting the AI sector. While Scassa sits on Champagne's AI advisory council, she did not join fellow members who in April 2023 signed an open letter urging Parliament to rapidly move AIDA forward. (She has since said the government's proposed amendments make it a better bill.)

A month earlier, a group of policy researchers and rights organizations published their own open letter calling for MPs to vote the legislation down. AIDA "doesn't address the human-rights implications of algorithmic systems," says Christelle Tessono, a Montrealer who's currently a fellow at Princeton University's Center for Information Technology Policy. The provisions require an individual to prove they were personally affected by an AI system, but harms can be collective, she says. And unlike the EU's AI Act, it doesn't outright ban uses that are "inherently discriminatory or simply flawed," like live facial recognition technology.

Tessono helped craft the March 2023 letter with the International Civil Liberties Monitoring Group, an Ottawa-based umbrella body. Parliament is advancing AIDA but signatories are still looking for the government to hear and address concerns. "First we want public consultation," says Ana Branducescu, a doctoral candidate at McGill University, calling for ISED to fund town halls across the country to discuss the proposed law in addition to more online methods.

The explorers

Jeff Clune et al. (University of British Columbia)

The federal government's $568.8-million Pan-Canadian AI Strategy devotes a significant share of its dollars to bringing top researchers to the country and keeping them here, in part so that they can train more algorithmically conversant graduates. Jeff Clune and his UBC lab are a case in point.

The computer scientist had stints at OpenAI and Uber before the university appointed him to its faculty in January 2021. His research focuses on advancing and analyzing neural networks, using evolutionary biology as a guide.

Clune's UBC lab is working on "open-ended learning," says Jenny Zhang, a first-year PhD student there—systems that set themselves new challenges and gain new skills, in a continuous-improvement loop. One aim is to help an AI agent "automatically update its environment in a way that's suitable for learning in the most efficient way," says Zhang. Her own work focuses on getting machines to innovate like people do, using the very human habit of pursuing interesting tasks and avoiding boring ones.

The lab is also exploring the technology's downsides. "We are quite concerned about AI existential risk and how AI will impact society," says Zhang. Clune has chronicled algorithmic systems doing unexpected—and sometimes problematic—things to meet their programmed objectives. Another researcher in the lab is working on ways to get an AI agent to explain what it is trying to achieve before taking an action, so it can be prevented from one that's potentially dangerous.

After an undergraduate degree at Imperial College London, Zhang chose UBC for the chance to work with Clune, whose prior research matched her interests. Drawing both professor and PhD student to the country is the kind of story the AI strategy was intended to produce.

Sanja Fidler (University of Toronto)

To figure out how to deal with the things in the real world around them, machines need to know what and where they are. Sanja Fidler's computer-vision research has long focused on such object-detection problems, even as she's trying to make it easier for AI systems and the humans that command them to talk to one another.

After getting her PhD at the University of Ljubljana, Fidler arrived at U of T in February 2011 as a postdoctoral fellow. The following year, Hinton and two students published a seminal paper about classifying images using neural nets. "All the eyes in the world turned to Toronto at the time," Fidler recalled. She's since helped the city attract and retain AI talent, supervising dozens of graduate and PhD students and co-founding the Vector Institute, opened in March 2017. Fidler's team has built tools for other researchers, like a system for data annotation and labelling.

She's also working on the industry side. In June 2018, Santa Clara's Nvidia announced it would open a Toronto AI research lab led by Fidler, who's now vice-president for the discipline across the company. Long a leader in graphics components for gamers, Nvidia has built a huge business in AI-specialized semiconductors. The products of the Toronto lab include a model released in September 2023 that generates 3D, animation-style renderings of buildings, animals, and other objects from flat images.

Fidler says U of T's willingness to let her hold corporate roles has contributed to the city's deep-learning boom. "Me and my students get to be part of academia . . . and at the same time we get the resources of industry and the insights and learnings of what's actually important in industry."

The wildcard

Ilya Sutskever (OpenAI)

Ilya Sutskever was born in Russia, grew up in Israel, immigrated to Canada as a teen, and in 2012, while studying under Geoffrey Hinton, contributed to the development of groundbreaking software that could identify the content of images by mimicking neural networks in the human brain.

After that massive breakthrough, Hinton reportedly auctioned off his team of researchers to the highest bidding tech company—which happened to be Google. Sutskever, who today is the third most-cited AI researcher in the world after Hinton and Bengio, left the search giant in 2015 to co-found OpenAI, where he took the role of chief scientist.

The founders of OpenAI dreamed of creating artificial general intelligence—as smart as or smarter than human beings—and ensuring that it would act in the best interests of humanity. Sutskever was part of a group of staff particularly concerned with the hypothetical existential risks posed by artificial general intelligence, co-leading a "superalignment" team to ensure the systems they were creating would share human values.

Sutskever led the famous November 2023 push to oust Altman, informing the former CEO of his termination via video chat on a Friday, reading from a script. By the following Monday morning, he'd had a change of heart, posting on X that he deeply regretted his actions and was joining more than 700 OpenAI employees in signing an open letter calling on the board—which Sutskever sat on at the time—to resign. Two days later, OpenAI announced Altman had been reinstated, saying in a blog post later that month that he had "love and respect" for Sutskever and was working to keep him at the company.

It's still not clear what led to the boardroom drama—theories include safety concerns, tension over Altman's other ventures and a diminished role for Sutskever. Regardless, the stakes are extremely high. At minimum, the fate of a company on track to be valued at US$86 billion hung in the balance. And if you believe Sutskever and those who think like him, the fate of humanity, too.

GIVE A THOUGHTFUL GIFT

GET THE <u>WHOLE</u> STORY